Dilemmas and Decision Making in Nursing

Other books you may be interested in:

Academic Writing and Referencing for your Nursing Degree
Jane Bottomley and Steven Pryjmachuk   ISBN 978-1-911106-95-1

Communication Skills for your Nursing Degree
Jane Bottomley and Steven Pryjmachuk   ISBN 978-1-912096-65-7

Critical Thinking Skills for your Nursing Degree
Jane Bottomley and Steven Pryjmachuk   ISBN 978-1-912096-69-5

Learning Disability Nursing
Ruth Northway and Paula Hopes   ISBN 978-1-914171-35-2

Psychopharmacology, Second Edition
Herbert Mwebe   ISBN 978-1-914171-44-4

Studying for your Nursing Degree
Jane Bottomley and Steven Pryjmachuk   ISBN 978-1-911106-91-3

To order our books please go to our website www.criticalpublishing.com or contact our distributor Ingram Publisher Services, telephone 01752 202301 or email IPSUK.orders@ingramcontent.com. Details of bulk order discounts can be found at www.criticalpublishing.com/delivery-information.

Our titles are also available in electronic format: for individual use via our website and for libraries and other institutions from all the major ebook platforms.

CRITICAL
PUBLISHING

Dilemmas and Decision Making in Nursing

A practice-based approach

Edited by
Julia Hubbard

First published in 2023 by Critical Publishing Ltd

British Library Cataloguing in Publication Data
A CIP record for this book is available from the British Library

ISBN: 978-1-915080-32-5

This book is also available in the following e-book formats:
EPUB ISBN: 978-1-915080-33-2
Adobe e-book ISBN: 978-1-915080-34-9

Cover and text design by Out of House Limited
Project management by Newgen Publishing UK
Printed and bound in Great Britain by 4edge, Essex

Critical Publishing
3 Connaught Road
St Albans
AL3 5RX

Printed on FSC
accredited paper

www.criticalpublishing.com

Dedication

This book is dedicated to those who devote their lives to nursing.

Acknowledgement

Grateful thanks to Abbi Jackson for kind permission to use the decision-making pitfalls table from her book *Dilemmas and Decision Making in Social Work* (2021, Critical Publishing).

Contents

Meet the editor and contributors   ix

Introduction   1

PART 1: PERCEPTIONS OF RISK AND SAFETY   5

Case study 1   Reuben: fit for discharge but not safe to leave   7
Joe Ellis-Gage

Case study 2   Miguel: is he safe?   15
Christine Nightingale

**Case study 3   Sabina: what's safeguarding got to do with me?
I am training to be a nurse not a social worker**   25
Katie Mclaughlin

Case study 4   Vanessa: coercion, control and personal choice   35
Sarah Housden

Case study 5   Martin: do no harm   45
Rebekah Hill

PART 2: PRIORITISING CARE   57

Case study 6   Molly: cold not dead   59
Joe Ellis-Gage

Case study 7   James: to donate or not to donate?   67
Joe Ellis-Gage

Case study 8   Aiyana: for crying out loud!   77
Sarah Housden

Case study 9   Peter: don't miss the point   89
Sally Hardy

Case study 10   Scarlet: cutting, coping and compassion   101
Louise Cherrill and Sarah Housden

PART 3: PERSONALISING CARE   117

Case study 11   **Stephanie: see me, hear me, include me**   119
Sally Hardy

Case study 12   **Jamil: false hope?**   127
Rebekah Hill

Case study 13   **Jessica: what matters most**   137
Emma Harris

Case study 14   **Roger: a case of mistaken reality**   149
Sarah Housden

Case study 15   **Lucy: the man I plan to marry**   157
Katrina Emerson

Conclusion   167

References   171

Index   185

Meet the editor

Julia Hubbard

Julia Hubbard is Professor of Clinical Health Education at the University of East Anglia (UEA) and a highly experienced academic having worked in university-level healthcare education since 1993. During this time, Julia has been involved in curriculum development and course delivery across a range of healthcare professions both at undergraduate and postgraduate levels, nationally and internationally. Her current roles include Director of Innovation and New Business, School of Health Sciences, University of East Anglia, which involves seeking out new education opportunities to meet the changing healthcare needs of the UK population. She is also Director of International Partnerships at the School of Health Sciences, University of East Anglia, where she works with and establishing new global education networks.

Meet the contributors

Louise Cherrill is a registered mental health nurse with experience in adult community mental health services, youth community mental health services, and triage and assessment (front door) for adult community mental health services. She has recently completed her intensive training in dialectical behavioural therapy. Louise is also a postgraduate researcher at UEA, completing her PhD studies on prevention and management of self-harming behaviours in young people. She is a visiting speaker for UEA, sharing her research knowledge and her experiences of service improvement in this area.

Joe Ellis-Gage is a registered children's nurse with extensive experience working in the emergency department. He has worked in both child and adult settings as an emergency nurse practitioner and was the clinical manager of a children's emergency department. Joe also spent time working as a specialist nurse in organ donation, working across the east of England co-ordinating organ donations while caring for end-of-life patients and their families. Joe is now a lecturer in children's nursing at UEA and the course director of the BSc children's nursing programme. He has a particular interest in simulation teaching.

Katrina Emerson is a registered adult health nurse and has worked for many years in sexual health and HIV as a sexual health/HIV specialist practitioner planning and delivering care and services in a variety of acute and community settings. This involved liaising with health and social care colleagues and the voluntary sector to co-ordinate services for service users, carers and their families. Katrina has worked with adults and children with HIV, and in collaboration with the HIV nursing team was instrumental in developing a range of specialist HIV nurse lead services. More recently, Katrina has been focusing on reproductive and sexual health.

Sally Hardy is Professor of Mental Health and Practice Innovation at the UEA, currently leading a large programme of work with the Integrated Care System in Norfolk and Waveney. She has worked within healthcare as a practitioner, researcher and educator for 40 years, bringing a wealth of experience to workforce and system transformation at the local, national and international levels.

Emma Harris is a registered adult nurse and has worked in acute medicine, urology and general surgery, and she specialised in colorectal and upper gastroenterology care. Before joining the UEA, Emma held a specialist palliative care role in the NHS and was project lead for Norfolk, implementing end-of-life education. Emma is an advanced communication skills facilitator for East Anglia, a role she has carried out for over 20 years. She also leads the UEA's foundations of end-of-life care module at BSc and MSc levels.

Rebekah Hill is a registered adult nurse who has worked in the clinical fields of acute medicine, critical care and gastroenterology/hepatology for many years. Rebekah now works as an associate professor and director of education in the School of Health Sciences at UEA. Rebekah completed her PhD on the experience of living with hepatitis C and continues to work closely with gastroenterology and hepatology specialty groups.

Sarah Housden is Associate Professor in Health Sciences at UEA. She has worked in education and practice with older people for over 20 years, specialising in promoting healthy ageing, and enhancing well-being in the context of dementia and/or frailty. As an educator she is passionate about providing learning opportunities that are inclusive and which use interactive approaches to engage health and care practitioners in actively improving their communication skills for working positively with stressed, distressed and vulnerable adults.

Katie Mclaughlin is an Associate Professor at the UEA and a Senior Fellow of the Higher Education Academy. She is an experienced registered health visitor and has worked in various roles, including as a safeguarding children's trainer in both primary care trusts and in a local commissioning group. This interest in child protection led her to work as a specialist nurse for safeguarding children. She is also a registered practice teacher for specialist community public health nursing and has a Master's degree in childcare law. Her research interests include female genital mutilation in diaspora communities, child exploitation, as well as public health and maternal health and child health.

Christine Nightingale is an Associate Dean of the Faculty of Medicine and Health Sciences at the UEA. A learning disability nurse by background Christine has worked across the NHS, commissioning, education and higher education sectors promoting equality, equity and inclusion. Her research has focused on sexual health, health inequalities for people with learning disabilities, mental health, disabled staff working in post-16 education and embedding equality and diversity into education. She is a nominated Fellow of the Royal Society of Arts and a Senior Fellow of the Higher Education Academy.

Introduction

Julia Hubbard

The aims of the book

This book highlights the incredible complexity of the skilled decision making undertaken by nurses working across diverse settings in the UK today. Exploring the dilemmas typically embedded in decision-making processes and experienced by nurses on a regular basis, the book will assist you in preparing for working with people across age ranges, as well as with their families, carers and other health and social care professionals. Through a series of case studies, the book provides opportunities to consider responses to professional dilemmas that you may not yet have experienced in your own practice, and through these to uncover new theories that will help you with decision making going forward. The aim of the book is to illustrate not only the complexity of decision making in nursing, but also of the context and culture of wider society, and of organisations within which such decisions are made. As you will see, nurses not only provide support and guidance for those under their care but consistently use their expertise and knowledge to co-ordinate care within the multidisciplinary team.

The role and scope of the work of the nurse is growing, with contexts of employment including settings such as hospitals, health centres, nursing homes, hospices, communities and academia. As nurses, we work across all demographics – adults, children, mental health and learning disability – usually in multidisciplinary teams; however, increasingly nurses are working independently. Understandably, not all interactions with the public are uncomplicated, and nurses need to be skilled in working within and across multi-professional and multi-agency teams (NMC, 2018a). For example, an individual with a condition requiring palliative care may be supported by a medical team with care delivered through a community palliative care hub. The pivotal point of contact, however, remains the nurse. The decision making in this model reflects a partnership approach and is often described as 'person-centred care', the importance of which is highlighted throughout this book.

Understandably, education and preparation for clinical practice is key. The standards of proficiency for registered nurses (NMC, 2018a) are grouped around seven platforms, which reflect what the nursing profession expects a newly registered nurse to know and do safely and proficiently at the start of their career. These NMC (Nursing and Midwifery Council) standards have been used to underpin the contents of this book. The case scenarios therefore aim to support your personal and professional development, including for those working towards professional registration. These standards are:

1. being an accountable professional;

2. promoting health and preventing ill health;

3. assessing needs and planning care;

4. providing and evaluating care;

5. leading and managing nursing care and working in teams;

6. improving quality of care;

7. co-ordinating care.

In addition to the above NMC standards of proficiency, the case studies in this book exhibit how the organisation and context of nursing care is changing because of the NHS Long Term Plan and the development of new nursing roles. The NHS Long Term Plan (NHS England, 2019) sets out a new service model for the twenty-first century and as such provides the context for the book's content. This plan responds to concerns about NHS funding, staffing, increasing health inequalities and pressures from a growing and ageing population. This has had various implications for nursing, including identifying the need to change our activity and challenge established practice, because services need to be delivered better, while striving for high-value care. In response to these challenges, this book explores current nursing practice through the presentation of a diverse range of fictional but true-to-life case studies, told from the perspective of the nurse. The authors' personal reflections on each case study explore best practice and take account of other healthcare professionals' perspectives, including challenges and barriers to multidisciplinary working. Key themes running through the book include:

• reflection;

• safeguarding;

• organisational culture;

• prioritisation of workload;

• human rights;

• healthcare values.

Structured into three key sections, the book progresses from considering perceptions of risk and safety through to prioritising care, and finally to examining how care can be personalised.

1. **Perceptions of risk and safety** when working with vulnerable individuals are explored with Reuben (child abuse), Miguel (neglect of health needs), Sabina (domestic abuse), Vanessa (coercion) and Martin (potential harm during research participation). These cases highlight that vulnerable individuals may present at any point of contact with healthcare professionals, emphasising the constant need to be alert to, and to raise, safeguarding concerns.

2. **Prioritising care** may differ depending on your point of view: that is, the individual receiving the care, their families and carers or the needs of the organisation. Molly (resuscitation following drowning), James (organ donation), Aiyana (perceived disruptive behaviour), Peter (overshadowing) and Scarlet (self-harm) provide a range of common dilemmas where consideration of all facts and points of view is key to appropriate and effective decision making.

3. **Personalising care** respects the wants and needs of the individual in our care when difficult conversations are needed. Stephanie (balancing a cultural context), Jamil (breaking bad news), Jessica (informed choice), Roger (enhancing sense of self) and Lucy (non-judgemental care) typify the complex situations in which nurses may find themselves.

How to use this book

This book can be read in several ways. Readers are invited to work through the case studies in the order of presentation, or to dip in and out of the case studies as free-standing sources of information matched to your specific learning requirements at any given time. Each case study starts with a fictitious but true-to-life clinical scenario told from the perspective of the nurse. These scenarios provide an insight into the various aspects of nursing practice and simultaneously impart nurses' underlying thinking and evidence-informed decision-making processes. Provided as distinct 'shoutouts' in the margins of the text, links are made with numerous approaches, values, models and theories which demonstrate how nurses make use of a wide range of tools and perspectives as part of appraising available options as they make robust clinical decisions in complex situations. These concepts are explained in more depth at the end of each scenario in a further information section.

The case studies also include nurses' reflections either in action (while it is happening) or on action (after the event), providing further insight into how clinical decisions must evolve based on the evidence available. A set of reflective questions then provide an opportunity for you to consider your own knowledge and learning. I hope that you find the questions stimulating and you take the opportunity to read further around the key areas of nursing practice.

In anticipation that you will want to relate your reading to your clinical practice, each case study provides some suggestions and resources to support further study. I would encourage you to work with either a peer or clinical supervisor to ensure you expose yourself to a variety of differing perspectives and analyse what you may, or may not, have done differently. By scrutinising, and reflecting on, day-to-day practice you will develop your understanding of the importance of being able to justify, sometimes to multiple audiences, the thinking and rationale underpinning your professional judgements.

Use the diagram in Figure 0.1 to help you work through the case studies in a systematic and considered way.

Finally, try looking through alternative lenses for each case. Such lenses could include, for example: age, gender, ethnicity, culture, religion, disability, trauma, domestic abuse, relationships, sexual orientation, learning needs, poverty, stigma, mental or physical health needs, carer status, personality, need/neglect, loss and grief, homelessness status, worldview or the views of other professionals (Jackson, 2021). Consider which lenses you could add to each scenario.

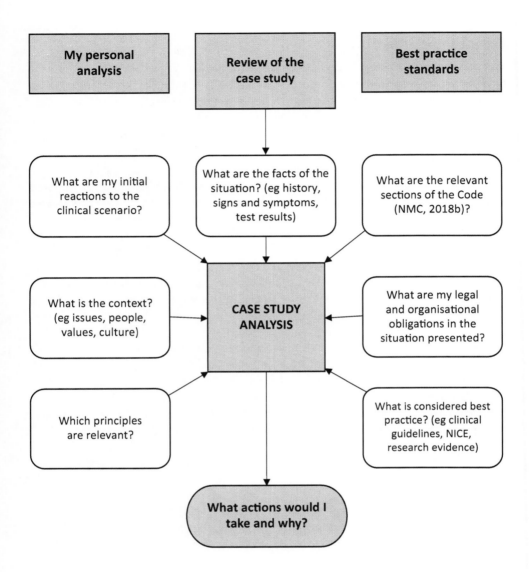

Figure 0.1 Reading the case studies

Part 1

Perceptions of risk and safety

Case study 1
Reuben: fit for discharge but not safe to leave

Joe Ellis-Gage

I was covering triage during a busy afternoon in the children's emergency department on the day I met Reuben. Children tend to be assessed in the order they arrive, but at busy times I like to scan the list of arrivals in case there is anyone waiting that needs prioritising. The usual things to keep an eye out for are complaints such as difficulty breathing or chest pain. On this day I notice a six-month-old baby has been booked in with the computer records system simply reading *unwell*, a generic term used by our receptionists when the presenting complaint is too broad or too tricky to classify. With such a vague presenting complaint and young age, I decide to call Reuben through.

Reuben is brought through by his mother, a tall, slim woman who I guess to be in her early forties. She looks anxious as she approaches and slightly frantic trying to get through to the triage room as quickly as she can. It is as if she thinks I might lose interest and call someone else in if she is not quick enough. I notice her appearance as it strikes me as being slightly odd; she is wearing what looks like expensive, high-quality clothes, but they are creased and mismatched.

Reuben is carried through in a car seat. I look inside and see him sleeping peacefully wrapped up in a cosy Winnie the Pooh snow-suit complete with bear ears. He looks clean and well cared for. The car seat is clearly expensive and well maintained.

'Come through, grab a seat.' I welcome them into the triage room. Before I can say anything more, Reuben's mother starts telling me why she is here. *'Reuben just hasn't been right today. He is usually such a happy baby, but today he has been irritable, won't take his milk and just keeps crying. I know nursery had a bug going round. I think he has that. I know he hasn't been sick yet, but if he has that bug and won't take his milk, he will end up dehydrated. I know that is not good for babies. They are so vulnerable...'*

'Okay – don't worry, we will take a look', I have to interject. *'Can I just take your name please?'*

'Elizabeth.'

VALUE: 'hello, my name is' campaign

'Okay Elizabeth, my name is Joe and I'm going to examine Reuben and see what we can do.' At this point I know this is going to take me longer than the average assessment. I ask Elizabeth to bring Reuben through to a side room and as we walk through, I quietly say to a colleague 'Could you cover triage for me? I don't want to rush this one'.

VALUE: teamwork

In the side room, I ask Elizabeth to lift Reuben from his car seat and remove his snow suit. Reuben wakes up, briefly looks shocked at the bright lights and unfamiliar surroundings but then looks straight at me and smiles. I briefly play peek-a-boo with him, hiding behind the observations chart I am holding before starting a structured assessment of airway, breathing and circulation, and then moving on to considering disability and exposure of Reuben. While carrying out the assessment, Elizabeth is telling me more.

APPROACH: gaining trust through play

MODEL: ABCDE assessment

'My husband, Ian, is an accountant with his own firm; his work is so busy at the moment that I don't want to distract him by telling him we are here. He would want to come over but would then have so much work to catch up on. I've told our other son, Seb, he's 15, but asked him not to mention it to his dad. Hopefully, we will be done before he finishes work.'

I think about this information for a minute. This mother is clearly worried about her baby and has genuine concerns for his well-being but does not want to tell the father. Surely he would want an update at least? I do not say anything, but my concerns are raised.

VALUE: intuition

The assessment of Reuben does not disclose any signs of him being unwell. His observations are normal, he appears well hydrated, there are no rashes, and he is alert and interested in his surroundings. There are, however, a couple of findings that worry me.

'Elizabeth, have you noticed these marks on Reuben?' I point to what I think is fingertip bruising on Reuben's upper arms. It looks old and is very faint. I also show Elizabeth a slightly raised red mark on Reuben's head, just in his hair line. This mark is about the size of pound coin and looks much more recent.

'No, I haven't. What are they? Are they the start of a rash? Is he okay?' Elizabeth says she does not know where the marks have come from. She is not at all defensive and appears to be worried. I explain the arms have signs of old bruising that we would not expect to see on a baby and that the mark on the head looks like a recent 'bump'. *'Do you recall him hitting his head at all?'*

Elizabeth does not recall a bump to the head. I reassure Elizabeth as I can see her anxiety is increasing again. I had gained her trust and was cautious that in this complex situation I did not want to lose it. I suggest we offer Reuben a feed and see how it goes. After that we will get Reuben reviewed by one of the doctors. I also suggest Elizabeth informs her husband so he can come to join them – I feel he may be able to support Elizabeth during this time. While Reuben is feeding I make sure I clearly document my assessment and concerns in the patient medical records.

APPROACH: therapeutic relationships

APPROACHES: family-centred care; accurate documentation

The feed goes well. Reuben takes it all and does not vomit. He appears content and sleepy after the feed, and Elizabeth looks more relaxed too. The doctor comes to see Reuben and I leave them to it. The department is getting busy, and I need to get back to triage. I am aware that while I have been in here the team have been covering for me. I return to triage and begin assessing the new arrivals: two clearly broken arms and a severe abdominal pain among many others. Before I know it, over an hour has passed. I want to know what the doctor thinks about Reuben. Were they concerned by the bruises? Did they find anything else in their examination? I find the doctor and ask for an update.

'He looks fine to me. He's fed, all obs normal. I've told them to stay for a while so we can observe, but they will hopefully go home later. Dad is on the way in too.'

'What did you think of the bruising and the bump on the head?'

'I saw the bump. Not sure what it is from, but these things happen to kids. They are always bumping something. I didn't see any bruises.'

'The fingertip bruising on the arms. Didn't you read my initial assessment? I documented about the bruises, the head bump and my concerns around the mum's demeanour.'

'Oh, no I didn't read anything. I just went straight in to see them. They seem like a nice family from a good home – I don't think it will be anything to worry about.'

THEORY: unconscious bias

I am frustrated. Children do often have bumps but not unwit-
nessed head injuries in immobile babies. I feel the doctor's
approach is a bit blasé. How had they missed the bruises? At
this point I notice a smart-looking man arrive in the department
and talk to the receptionist before being shown through to the
side room – Reubens' dad, Ian. I smile a 'hello' as he enters and
then allow them a bit of time together.

Just a few minutes later, Elizabeth comes out and asks to speak
with me.

*'I've remembered what happened that explains the bump on the
head. Yesterday we were unpacking the supermarket shopping
and Seb was helping me. Reuben was asleep in his car seat on the
floor. Seb was trying to carry too much at once and as he passed
Reuben he dropped a bag of carrots that landed straight on him.
He cried for a bit but quickly settled down. So that explains it –
nothing to worry about! We are really reassured – thank you for
being so thorough and kind. I'm happy to take him home now; we
won't take up anymore of your time.'*

She turns and heads back into the room to get ready to leave.
I am extremely uncomfortable with this situation as there are too
many unanswered questions and red flags. Elizabeth has gone
from an extremely anxious mother with no recollection of an
injury to being completely relaxed and remembering what I think
sounds like a made-up head injury. I follow Elizabeth into the
room and say I would like them to stay a little while longer so
we could reassess Reuben before they go. I was hoping to buy
myself some time.

*'Reuben looks fine to me. If you want to check him over, you can
have a look at him now'*, Ian replies. He is firm yet relaxed.

*'It isn't just a physical examination that we need to do. I'm worried
about the bruises on his arms and I'm not happy that the story
matches up about the bump on the head'*, I blurt it all out. It was
not the most tactful approach, but I have clearly expressed my
concerns.

I leave the room and go to speak to the doctor. *'I don't know what
to do'*, she says. *'I could refer to paediatrics for a review with
concerns about safeguarding, but I am not sure they are going to
agree with that. In fact, is that not them leaving right now?'*

I turn and see both parents leaving with the father carrying the car seat. The department doors are locked but as they approach the doors someone comes in and opens the door so they can walk straight out. I call after them and ask them to wait, but the door swings shut behind them.

I think about what to do next. Should I try to stop them? Even if I had a good reason, how would I do it? At that point I decide that although I have safeguarding concerns, I do not think the child is in immediate risk. I do not have grounds to stop the family leaving. I document my concerns, contact the trust safeguarding team for guidance and make a referral to children's services. My instinct may be wrong but a referral at this point is in the best interests of Reuben. They told me the child is not known to them – so there are no active concerns already – but that they would follow it up and contact the family. And that was it; they did not require anything else from me and they were happy to follow it up from here. I spent the rest of my shift assessing the other arrivals to the department while thinking about Reuben and Elizabeth.

APPROACH: child-centred approach to safeguarding

Reflections

This situation played on my mind for some time after. The only update I got was that the family were receiving input from children's services. There were many unanswered questions.

I think back to my initial assessment of Reuben. Was there anything I had missed? I did not think so; I had been thorough. But what if I had missed something more serious – would that have changed the children's services outcome?

I think back to the moment Ian arrived. This was when the situation changed. I really do not know if he had been abusive to Reuben, but my gut instinct was that he was coercive and controlling of Elizabeth. From the moment he arrived, her behaviour changed. There are clear links between coercive control and physical or sexual violence (Stark and Hester, 2018) so taking this seriously is essential. At that point I wonder if I should have been more forward in my questioning of Elizabeth. If I had taken her aside and asked her directly if Ian made her feel unsafe, what would she have said? Experience tells me she would have denied everything but at least I would have tried. Or maybe I should have spent more time with Ian? Would that have given me a clearer

THEORY: coercive control

THEORY: adverse childhood experiences

view on the situation? I think about the potential long-term impact on Reuben of being subject to domestic abuse. The impact of traumatic events on children can be significant for both their physical and mental health throughout their life.

Why had the doctor been so relaxed and dismissive of my concerns? I knew this doctor well and they were good. In fact, I can recall a previous safeguarding issue where they were pro-active and worked in the best interests of a child. Why was this case different? It could have been that the situation was not as clear. It could have been because it was a busy shift and other things took priority. But my instinct was that this was missed because Elizabeth, Ian and Reuben did not look like your *average safeguarding concerns family*. This family were well spoken, well presented and well off. Ian had a responsible job. Elizabeth spoke well, with a well-to-do accent. Reuben was in expensive, clean clothes. I worry that the doctor did not raise concerns because this family were middle class.

I also wonder if we had a system failure. Infants with bruising like this should be seen by an expert (The Child Safeguarding Practice Review Panel, 2022). The emergency department doctor was not an expert, and they dismissed my concerns when Reuben should have been examined again to be sure and referred to a paediatrician for review. I had not been firm enough with the doctor. I should have told them Reuben needed a referral. I will not make that mistake again.

Questions for reflection and discussion

1. How can emergency departments be more proactive in supporting victims of domestic abuse to speak out?

2. How could staff benefit from unconscious bias training in relation to safeguarding?

3. Why are safeguarding concerns raised more in certain groups of patients?

4. How could this situation have been managed differently to ensure the safety of the child was maintained?

5. What are the most common signs and symptoms of abuse in infants, and how do they differ from signs and symptoms in older children?

6. How could outcomes of children's services referrals be shared with emergency department staff and how would such feedback better inform their practice?

Further information

VALUES

Intuition An understanding of something based on instinct rather than fact. However, clinical intuition is understood to be based on knowledge and experience rather an unexplained feeling (Melin-Johansson et al, 2017).

'Hello, my name is' campaign A campaign to improve person-centred, compassionate care with a focus on all healthcare staff introducing themselves to patients in their first interaction. You can find out more about this at: www.hellomynameis.org.uk

Teamwork Within emergency departments, teamwork has been noted to reduce errors, increase staff satisfaction, improve operational activity and benefit patient outcomes (Grover et al, 2017).

THEORIES

Unconscious bias Attitudes towards a particular group based on stereotypes that impact the way the group is treated (Veesart and Barron 2020).

Coercive control The ongoing behaviour of one person towards another that includes threatening and controlling behaviour. Often linked to negative outcomes of children in relationships where there is coercive control (Stark and Hester, 2018).

Adverse childhood experiences Traumatic experiences during childhood. Exposure to a number of these events during childhood has been shown to lead to long-term negative physical and mental health outcomes (Boullier and Blair, 2018).

APPROACHES

Gaining trust through play Adapting behaviour to interact with a child in a way which they relate to and as a result their confidence in you develops.

Therapeutic relationships Positive nurse–patient interactions based around trust. Linked to improved patient experience and outcomes (Akyirem et al, 2022).

Family-centred care Involving patients and their families in the planning of their care to ensure mutually agreeable goals.

Accurate documentation Clear, accurate record keeping, including but not limited to patient medical records (NMC, 2018b).

Safeguarding children Promoting welfare, best outcomes and preventing maltreatment (HM Government, 2018).

Child-centred approach to safeguarding Ensuring the child is the primary focus when decisions around safeguarding are made (HM Government, 2018).

MODELS

ABCDE assessment A structured assessment model to ensure all patients receive the same treatment and nothing major is missed. This includes an assessment of Airway, Breathing, Circulation, Disability and Exposure (Resuscitation Council UK, 2015).

Further reading

Arthurs, O, Williams, D and Steele, A (2021) Safeguarding Children: Are We Getting It Right? *Archives of Disease in Childhood*, 107(9): 777–8.

Early Intervention Foundation (2020) *Adverse Childhood Experiences: What We Know, What We Don't Know, and What Should Happen Next*. London: Early Intervention Foundation.

Hung, K L (2020) Pediatric Abusive Head Trauma. *Biomedical Journal*, 43(3): 240–50.

Johnson, E, Jones, A and Maguire, S (2021) Bruising: The Most Common Injury in Physical Child Abuse. *Paediatrics and Child Health*, 31(11): 403–9.

National Society for the Prevention of Cruelty to Children (2015) *Paediatrics and Accident and Emergency: Learning from Case Reviews*. [online] Available at https://learning.nspcc.org.uk/research-resources/learning-from-case-reviews/paediatrics-accident-emergency (accessed 23 February 2023).

Case study 2
Miguel: is he safe?

Christine Nightingale

It was Monday morning and I was checking the messages that had come in on the system over the weekend. As a community learning disability nurse, I work in a multidisciplinary team (MDT) with registered learning disability nurses (RNLD), a speech and language therapist, a psychologist, social workers and healthcare assistants. I had a lengthy list of nursing interventions to plan and deliver that week, including supporting families in identifying future options for their disabled child, making a dementia assessment of an older woman with learning disabilities who lived in sheltered housing and developing a programme of work on supporting women with learning disabilities to make an informed choice on breast and cervical screening. I was hoping that there had been no concerns reported to the weekend social services duty officer. Among the usual messages, there was an email with a password-protected attachment which caught my eye, sent by practice nurse Jac at one of the health centres in the geographical area in which I work. On opening the attachment, I was struck by how clearly presented the message was using SBAR (situation, background, assessment and recommendation).

> **MODEL: multidisciplinary teams**

> **APPROACH: role of a learning disability nurse**

> **VALUE: confidentiality**

> **MODEL: SBAR model of communication**

The written email referral

Situation:

Hi Chris, this is Jac, practice nurse. I am messaging about Miguel H, who I see is known to your service but has not been actively seen, according to our records, for around a year. I need to report that he was booked for his Covid and flu vaccinations on Saturday morning but did not attend.

I phoned Miguel's home. The call was answered by Miguel, but when I asked about his vaccine appointment, someone who said he was Miguel's cousin came on the line. The 'cousin' said that Miguel did not like injections, so it was pointless bringing him. They also added that he has been overly aggressive recently, and it was not safe to take him out as his behaviour might place the health centre staff and the public at risk of injury. They then hung up.

I checked back on his notes and found that he is now six months overdue for his Covid boosters and late for his annual health check.

Background:

Miguel is a 42-year-old male patient registered at this practice. He has a learning disability, with functional verbal communication skills. He can express his likes and dislikes in short sentences and will reinforce this communication with gestures such as shaking or nodding his head.

I can see from previous notes on the system that Miguel has continued to live in his family home after his parents died, as he was assessed as having sufficient skills and understanding to keep himself safe, prepare meals (mostly using the microwave oven) and meet his friends for coffee.

Assessment:

I am puzzled as previous notes suggest a different personality and behavioural outlook than was suggested to me this weekend. Our notes also refer to the need for best interest discussions before interventions such as phlebotomy as he has not shown evidence of sufficient capacity to agree to the procedure.

I am increasingly concerned for this man's safety. I am worried that he has not had the opportunity for an annual health check or entered fully into a vaccination programme, placing him at risk of an infectious disease or a late diagnosis of another health condition. The report from the 'cousin' that Miguel is displaying distressed behaviour appears to be out of character.

Recommendation:

Please could your team identify whether there have been any changes in Miguel's life that may explain the missed appointments, and whether we should be concerned about the 'cousin'.

- *Assess any behaviour changes, particularly those that may require us at the health centre to change our approach.*

- *Identify a plan to encourage Miguel into the health centre for his vaccinations and annual health check so we can eliminate any physical or medical changes.*

- *I will place a temporary warning notice on his notes, so that if Miguel or anyone said to be representing him make contact, the call will be escalated immediately to myself on the on-duty doctor.*

I am on duty on Monday afternoon if you would like to discuss this further.

Kind regards, Jac.

Having read this referral, my task was now to weigh up the information, check our files for any further information and form a plan of action.

It is fair to say that I almost dismissed the referral when I thought it was just reporting one missed vaccine appointment. I was at first not overly concerned; after all, like anyone else he may have forgotten or been feeling unwell. However, Jac had added that this was not the first time that Miguel had missed an appointment for his Covid vaccination. I knew that across all life stages people with learning disabilities have been the most negatively impacted by the first wave of Covid-19 and experienced the highest proportional death rate from the disease. Campaigners had fought to get people with learning disabilities recognised as highly vulnerable and be prioritised for Covid vaccinations regardless of their age.

THEORY: health inequalities

Over my years as a learning disability nurse, I had witnessed the shorter life expectancy of people with learning disabilities, who had died of diagnosable diseases and treatable conditions. Miguel had not had his yearly learning disability health check. This missed annual review had not been previously reported to the community nurses and multidisciplinary team (MDT), but shamefully for us we had not spotted this omission either.

THEORY: health inequalities

VALUE: accountability

I agreed with Jac that a number of physiological assessments would be useful, as well as a plan to achieve an annual health check and vaccine. While, in the past, mental capacity assessments had indicated that Miguel was not able to weigh up or repeat information about specific interventions such as vaccines and blood tests, he had not resisted any of these procedures following agreement via a best interest conversation with a trusted and appointed advocate.

THEORY: Mental Capacity Act, 2005

Jac had found that a person, apparently unknown to the services who supported Miguel, may be having some influence on his life. I thought I ought to check this, and so I called Miguel's case file up on the system. There were no known surviving relatives.

Jac had cited the 'cousin' as saying that Miguel was aggressive and a risk to their own and others' safety. I had met Miguel in the past; my own experience, backed up by the care notes suggested that displays of aggression were completely out of character. This reported behaviour had not been witnessed or reported by any of the services Miguel encountered, and so could only be considered as alleged changes at this stage. High-profile reports have shown that people with learning disabilities are highly susceptible to coercive control and targeting by criminals.

I had to confront the uneasy thought that this reported aggressive behaviour was because of physical pain or psychological distress, and that it was imperative to assess Miguel as soon as possible. This was troubling, as evidence has shown that a reason why people with a learning disability are often not diagnosed with treatable or manageable conditions in a timely manner is because of diagnostic overshadowing. Further health inequalities and direct and indirect discrimination of people with learning disabilities in the health and social care system are associated with poor diagnostic practice.

I was imagining the worst possible interpretation of this complex situation. He was a vulnerable person, protected by safeguarding legislation. I needed to act quickly to determine whether Miguel was at risk from a form of abuse, being exploited or controlled. Indeed, failing to support a person with a learning disability to attend their essential health appointments could be considered as an act of neglect. I had two conflicting professional challenges. The first was my urge to go immediately and by myself to visit Miguel in his home to alleviate my concerns. The second was knowing that I should adhere to safeguarding protocol, which might mean delaying a visit while the safeguarding team decided whether to involve their trained investigators or the police. I knew that if I visited, knowing that a coercive person could be present, I could place Miguel at further risk and could prejudice any investigations into his safety. Seeking guidance and advice from the safeguarding team would be my first action.

As expected, the central safeguarding team were very responsive and efficient. I was promised an answer from them within the next few hours and in the meantime was advised to continue to prepare the assessments and plans for supporting Miguel whatever the outcome of the safeguarding investigation might be.

Reflections

Now that there had been a few weeks since I received the email from Jac, I had reflected on the hours I spent that Monday morning reacting to the referral. I thought about my range of emotions and feelings as I read Jac's email and of the way I was able to draw on theory, policy and evidence when considering what actions I might take.

My emotional reactions took me by surprise. Initially, I was slightly irritated at what I thought was an implied criticism, from Jac, that Miguel had not been seen by our service for a while. I had been aware of being distracted by having thoughts of *'what does Jac know about how we manage the complexity of our caseloads?'* As the detail of the referral became more complex, I was aware that I felt fear; it is important to understand the reasons for emotional reactions as these might be significant, at the same time understanding that emotions could also negatively influence the way in which I read and engaged with this referral.

THEORY: emotional intelligence

In reflecting on the ways in which evidence had influenced my thinking, I was pleased to be able to consider the theories of coercive control, diagnostic overshadowing and health inequalities in my critical reading of this referral. As I have mentioned, there have been shameful reports on the inequalities experienced by people with learning disabilities in accessing health and social care, including of untimely death and undiagnosed illnesses. I felt I had always been diligent and a strong advocate for the people I supported in getting full access to services, yet here I was with a man on my caseload who had missed appointments. I felt ashamed, wanting in my practice and remorseful. I recognised that communication systems can fail, and that I needed to work with our multidisciplinary team to conduct a root cause analysis of how Miguel's missed appointment had escaped us and to plan to prevent this from happening again.

MODEL: problem identification

I have been a registered nurse for many years, yet each day I find that there are opportunities to reflect on my practice, to learn from things that went well and things that did not go so well, and to apply evidence and findings from reports and research to my everyday work.

Questions for reflection and discussion

1. How can we as nurses best identify and respond to our emotional reactions to how other people speak to or behave towards us?

2. Explain what would have been your initial thoughts and nursing plan if the situation was less complicated and this was a genuinely forgotten appointment.

3. How and to what extent has the Code (NMC, 2018b) been demonstrated in this case study and reflection?

4. In this case study, the practice nurse recommended that the community learning disability nurse should make a home visit and conduct physical and social/environmental assessments. To what extent can a registered nurse or other registered practitioner delegate to another registered practitioner?

5. Why are people with learning disabilities considered to be 'vulnerable'?

   • To what extent do you think Miguel was at risk?

   • Using the Care Act 2014 definitions of abuse, identify where the risks of abuse could lie for Miguel.

6. Identify and read a paper about 'diagnostic overshadowing'. For example, Javaid et al (2019) 'Diagnostic overshadowing in learning disability: Think beyond the disability'. Reflect on how people in your care who may have a learning disability, psychosis, dementia or a degenerative or brain injury could be subject to diagnostic overshadowing.

Further information

VALUES

Confidentiality This is enshrined in the NHS Constitution (Department of Health & Social Care, 2021), which pledges that patients and service users' information will be treated with dignity and respect and charges staff to protect the confidentiality of the personal information that they hold.

Timely referrals These should be used to preserve the safety of patients and service users. Nurses should make timely referrals to other practitioners when other skills and expertise are needed to expedite care and treatment (NMC 2018b).

Accountability The Nursing and Midwifery Council (NMC, nd) define accountability as *'the principle that individuals and organisations are responsible for their actions and may be required to explain them to others'*. To be accountable, nurses have the responsibility to ensure that when accepting, undertaking or delegating tasks they must have the ability to perform the task, accept responsibility for doing it and have the authority to do the task evidenced by delegation and the policies and protocols of the organisation that the nurse is working for.

Act without delay This is a clause within the preserve safety pillar of the Code (NMC, 2018b), which refers to taking action, and if necessary, escalating concerns about patient or public safety.

THEORIES

Health inequalities Defined by McCartney et al (2019, p 29) as *'the systematic, avoidable and unfair differences in health outcomes that can be observed between populations, between social groups within the same population'*. Investigations have shown the considerable health inequalities resulting in untimely deaths of people with learning disabilities (Mencap, 2007).

Mental Capacity Act 2005 A law which empowers people to make decisions for themselves and protects those who lack the capacity to decide by providing a flexible framework that places individuals at the heart of the decision-making process (Social Care Institute for Excellence, 2022).

Distressed behaviours These are behaviours that might be considered physically aggressive that people may display as a response to emotional fear, when they are finding it difficult to get their needs met, are in pain or experiencing difficulties in understanding a change in routine or circumstances.

Socio-economic determinants of health Refer to the impact that community, family and financial environment can have on health and well-being. Wiseman and Watson (2022) investigated the negative social experiences of people with learning disabilities, finding social abuse, disrespect and devaluing behaviour to profoundly erode well-being.

Coercive control May involve influencing the behaviours of others by exerting psychological control, sometimes reinforced by abuse (Foundation for People with Learning Disabilities, 2018). Targeting practices can include the practice known as *'cuckooing'* where individuals not only coercively control vulnerable people but may also move into or use other people's property and resources without their legal consent.

Diagnostic overshadowing Can occur in situations where carers do not know the person very well, where an individual is vulnerable and has difficulty in making their needs understood, and where causes of distress or changes in behaviour are assumed to be expected for people with a learning disability. In other words, manifestations of pain including withdrawal, aggression, self-harm, crying and other distress signals are categorised as a symptom of a 'learning disability', dementia, autism or psychosis and so 'diagnostically overshadow' any other causes of the distressed behaviour (Javaid et al, 2019).

Care Act 2014 Enables identification of people with learning disabilities as 'vulnerable' and in need of safeguarding measures and protection from the many forms of abuse (Social Care Institute for Excellence, 2016).

Emotional intelligence A construct strongly debated by psychologists who question whether it is a personality trait or a skill that can be learnt. Mayer and Salovey (1997) define four branches of ability in emotionally intelligent people. They can: perceive the emotions of self and others; use emotions to facilitate thinking; understand emotional meanings in relationships; and manage emotions by promoting emotional and intellectual growth.

APPROACHES

Role of a learning disability nurse Encompasses several attributes and skills. Mason-Angelou (2020) summarises the definition of the learning disability nurse as: *'Learning disability nurses are nurses first and learning disability specialists second. They have the clinical skills of registered nurses combined with specialist learning disability knowledge. ... they have the clinical knowledge to ensure holistic care and treatment is provided within the context of someone with a learning disability's life. [Other skills] include being facilitators, educators, advocates, clinical experts, leaders, and mediators. These attributes, help prevent issues such as diagnostic overshadowing, health inequalities, premature deaths and inappropriate admissions.'*

Professional curiosity The intended outcome of professional curiosity is to avoid acting based on assumptions or untested information. Professional curiosity is vital when working with vulnerable children and adults and when there may be concerns about safety. Thacker et al (2019) refer to specific skills of deeper enquiry, proactive questioning and respectful challenge to exercise professional responsibility and know when to act.

Delegation A formal process in healthcare and is defined *'as the transfer to a competent individual, of the authority to perform a specific task in a specified situation'* (NMC, nd). As mentioned in the definition of accountability, where both the delegator and delegate are registered nurses both must understand their responsibilities in transferring and receiving the task and their responsibility to account for their actions.

Health review A recommended and proven route to identifying and tackling health inequalities (Cobb et al, 2008) for people over the age of 14 years who have a learning disability. The Learning Disabilities Mortality Review (Norah Fry Centre, 2021) stated that one of the several variables significantly associated with the likelihood of dying aged 18–49 years was failing to have an annual health check in the year preceding death.

MODELS

Multidisciplinary teams Characterised by having a group of professionals whose skills, knowledge and responsibilities can transcend professional boundaries and collectively ensure that there are seamless opportunities to address the care needs of the service user. Multidisciplinary teams were first introduced in the 1970s for people with learning disabilities in response to fragmented inaccessible services (Kelly, 2018).

SBAR model of communication This model of communicating vital information was originally developed by the US military. The four components: situation, background, assessment and recommendation, used skilfully, ensure that the key information is relayed between healthcare professionals. The approach not only encourages healthcare professionals to describe the situation but to also make an assessment and recommendations of what they wish the receiving healthcare professional to do (NHS England and NHS Improvement, nd b).

Problem identification Root cause analysis is a tool which supports the systematic analysis of a problem. Although not a suitable methodology for a serious incident, it is one way of looking into how and why things have happened and to identify better ways to provide safer care (NHS England and NHS Improvement, nd a).

Further reading

Cobb, J, Girauld, A and Kerr, M (2008) Health Checks and People with Learning Disability. *Tizard Learning Disability Review*. [online] Available at: www-emerald-com.uea.idm.oclc.org/insight/content/doi/10.1108/13595474200800028/full/pdf?title=health-checks-and-people-with-learning-disabilities (accessed 10 January 2023).

Javaid, A, Nakata, V and Dasari, M (2019) Diagnostic Overshadowing in Learning Disability: Think Beyond the Disability. *Progress in Neurology and Psychiatry*, 23(2): 8–10.

Mencap (2007) *Death by Indifference: 74 Deaths and Counting.* [online] Available at: www.mencap.org.uk/sites/default/files/2016-08/Death%20by%20Indifference%20-%2074%20deaths%20and%20counting.pdf (accessed 15 December 2022).

Norah Fry Centre (2021) *Learning Disabilities Mortality Review (LeDeR) programme (2020).* Annual Report. Bristol: University of Bristol. [online] Available at: https://leder.nhs.uk/images/annual_reports/LeDeR-bristol-annual-report-2020.pdf (accessed 15 December 2022).

Wiseman, P and Watson, N (2022) 'Because I've Got a Learning Disability, They Don't Take Me Seriously': Violence, Wellbeing, and Devaluing People with Learning Disabilities. *Journal of Interpersonal Violence*, 37(13/14).

Case study 3
Sabina: what's safeguarding got to do with me? I am training to be a nurse not a social worker

Katie Mclaughlin

As a student in the emergency department (ED), my placement has been challenging to say the least; just keeping up with the vast variety of patient presentations to the ED has been such a steep learning curve. My shift today begins with an allocation of a patient called Sabina. I quickly scan her notes and see that she is 22 years old. I immediately resonate with her as we are roughly the same age. I see from her medical records that Sabina has regularly attended ED with soft tissue damage and bruising. Today she is attending ED reporting she has fallen over her child's toy and hurt her left wrist. Sabina has also disclosed when she booked in at reception that she is 15 weeks pregnant with her second child.

I call Sabina's name in the waiting room. *'About bloody time – I've been waiting for ages'*, she grumbles as she tries to propel a pushchair containing a sleeping toddler towards me. I can see she is struggling as she is only able to use one hand. I smile as I take the pushchair handle to assist her: *'Here, let me help you; it must be hard to push this with your sore wrist'*. As we leave the waiting room, I hear Sabina's phone ping with a text message on which she now focuses all her attention. She replies to the text immediately, telling me casually, *'that's my fella – he wanted to know where I was; he's a bit overprotective and gets cross if I don't text him back immediately'*.

VALUE: empathy

THEORY: controlling behaviour

We go into a free cubicle in the minor injuries treatment area, and I introduce myself and explain her wrist will need to be examined by a doctor. She describes how she tripped up the stairs at home. This does not match the explanation given when she checked in, so I ask her to clarify this. Sabina appears flustered and avoids eye contact with me as she speaks: *'There was a toy on the stairs; I didn't see it. I tripped forwards and put out my hands, so I didn't face plant.'* I explain again that we will need to examine her wrist and she will need to have an X-ray to see if there is anything broken. Before I can tell her about the current wait time for treatment, her phone pings again with another text message and Sabina immediately disengages from our conversation and starts texting back. She looks up from her phone: *'It was him again; he texts me all the time now that I am having his baby.'* I repeat my earlier points about what needs to happen next and apologise that the department is very busy so the wait time might be several hours. At this, Sabina looks panic stricken and states in a trembling voice, *'I can't be too long! He will be angry if I take too long! Anyway, Daisy will be waking up soon'*. She pleads with me: *'Is there any way of speeding up the process?'*

Alarm bells begin to ring in my head. There is a clear discrepancy in her story relating to how the injury occurred, the frequent text messaging that consumes her attention and her concerns about the long waiting time. I had recently completed my safeguarding

VALUE: competence

APPROACH: recognising signs of abuse

training and recognise these as alerting factors for potential domestic abuse. I pluck up the courage to ask what she means by he will get cross and then ask whether he ever frightens her. Sabina explains that he can be short-tempered but that it is only because he is tired and works such long hours. *'He only gets*

VALUE: courage

MODEL: Duluth wheel of power and control

cross when I have done something wrong like being late home or not having his meal ready.'

THEORIES: domestic abuse; coercive control

'Your partner getting angry with you is not an okay response, Sabina. Have you ever heard the terms domestic abuse or coercive control?'

With that, Sabina gets angry and starts shouting, *'busy bodies like you should stop sticking their noses into other people's business'*. She says that she has just come today to get her wrist looked at and that I should get her seen and stop asking *'bloody stupid questions'*. She shouts at me that the midwife just asked her the same question and demands, *'what is it with you people?'* I try to de-escalate the situation and apologise that I upset her by

APPROACH: de-escalation

mentioning domestic abuse. I explain we see lots of people in the ED who are experiencing it, and I can signpost her to support such as the national domestic abuse helpline, Women's Aid or social care if she would like me to.

Again, this was the wrong thing to say to Sabina, who screams at me that *'there is no way that "the social" are going to be involved. I know my rights! You're not allowed to tell them I've been here today'*. I really need to seek help managing this situation so

VALUES: professionalism; raising concerns

I calmly say that I will go and check on the current waiting time for her and come straight back. I try to find my practice assessor and raise my concerns with her, but she is currently busy with a patient. I check the waiting times and return to Sabina's cubicle to find it is empty; the healthcare assistant tells me Sabina left saying that she could not wait to be seen.

My practice assessor finds me, and I inform her what has happened. She suggests that I contact the safeguarding team for advice. I am nervous about doing this as I wonder if I have jumped to conclusions and am wrong. However, I should not have worried. The process of safeguarding supervision with the safeguarding specialist nurse is helpful. They listen to what had happened and my concerns, including previous presentations at ED, the inconsistencies in Sabina's story, the repeated text messages and what she had said about her partner getting angry if she took too long. We talk about how bad I felt that Sabina had left the department without treatment. The safeguarding nurse explains that domestic abuse survivors may experience up to 35 instances of domestic abuse before seeking help.

MODEL: safeguarding clinical supervision

THEORY: cycle of repeated abuse

The safeguarding nurse then asks if Sabina had any dependents. We explore Sabina's pregnancy and young child and the increased vulnerability. I remembered reading the local trust policy on safeguarding children, which had included a definition of emotional abuse: 'seeing or hearing the ill-treatment of another'. It is clear a referral to children's social care (CSC) is required. This makes me feel uneasy as I assume that Sabina would have refused this and would see this as interference. What if my actions put Sabina in more danger? She had not consented to me sharing information and I had not told her about my concerns. I raise this potential ethical dilemma with the safeguarding nurse, who explains that the law justifies sharing information without consent in the 'public interest' in some situations, such as when children or others may be at risk.

THEORIES: child protection; emotional abuse

VALUE: assumptions

THEORY: consent

THEORY: information sharing

The safeguarding nurse assures me that my concerns are only a small part of the 'jigsaw' but, by sharing information with CSC, the risks to Sabina and her children could be assessed through a multi-agency approach with other professionals such as Sabina's midwife, health visitor and GP. The safeguarding nurse reminds me of the definition of domestic abuse provided by the National Institute for Health and Care Excellence (NICE, 2015), which includes not just physical harm but also controlling, coercive or threatening behaviour. Legally, the welfare of the child must be 'paramount'.

APPROACH: multi-agency working

APPROACH: paramountcy

Reflections

On reflection, I acknowledge my uncomfortable feelings as I ask myself if I approached the situation in the wrong way, causing Sabina to leave without receiving the care she might need. What if my own experience of domestic abuse made me jump to the wrong conclusions or make assumptions? Perhaps if I had spent more time with her and built a trusting, therapeutic relationship things may have turned out differently. Had I rushed in too quickly asking about domestic abuse? What if my actions had made things worse for Sabina? I am afraid that she might not access the ED again if she thinks she will be '*interrogated*'.

As a placement, the ED is fast moving and sometimes I get frustrated that there is not the time to spend with patients. The ED is widely recognised as a common healthcare facility where domestic abuse is often identified or disclosed. As a student nurse, I have the same duty as all healthcare professionals to

VALUE: duty of care to safeguard

safeguard all patients so needed to make more time to talk to Sabina. Effective communication skills are vital in nursing and I had not really had the chance to build a rapport with Sabina and

VALUE: communication skills

this is something I must remember to do much sooner, especially in my current fast-paced placement.

Reflecting more on Sabina's aggressive response to being asked about domestic abuse, it may not have been the way in which I had asked, but more a reflection of her denial or minimising of the abuse. What could be central to Sabina's behaviour with her leaving the ED without treatment might be symptomatic of her being afraid of her partner's coercive control. Coercive and controlling behaviour can be missed because it can masquerade as '*caring*' with survivors becoming so downtrodden that they do not identify that abuse is occurring. Sabina is also more vulnerable as she is pregnant and has a young child. If I had reworded my conversation and used open-

THEORIES: controlling behaviour; vulnerability; open questions

ended questions this might have helped Sabina to open up to me. To build my confidence, the use of routine questioning might help shape the way in which I ask the question. This is something to work on because as a nurse, I will have regular contact with people so I will be in an ideal position to recognise and respond to domestic abuse.

I had felt uneasy about sharing information with CSC without Sabina's consent, but by leaving, Sabina had not given me the chance to explain. If anything, her leaving added to my concerns. What I have learnt is to follow the policy and procedures and not to let the fear of damaging relationships get in the way of protecting children and adults, who may be at risk from abuse and neglect. The opportunity of having safeguarding supervision with the safeguarding lead was useful as they helped me voice my concerns but also supported me to make the referral and to complete all the documentation. It gave me confidence that I was doing what was expected of me and that I had shared information correctly in a way that was necessary, proportionate, relevant, adequate, accurate, timely and secure.

VALUE: record keeping

THEORY: information sharing

I recognise more now that safeguarding is complex and often not clear-cut so I will raise concerns with experienced colleagues or safeguarding leads as nurses have a key role in recognising safeguarding concerns and raising their concerns immediately if they think a person is vulnerable or at risk and needs extra support and protection (NMC, 2018b). Safeguarding is everyone's responsibility.

Questions for reflection and discussion

1. How might the situation have been handled if Sabina had not left the ED?

2. Should there be routine screening for domestic abuse in all healthcare settings? What might be the advantages or disadvantages of this?

3. Critically discuss good practice when making a referral to children's social care and consider what information you would share in this instance.

4. How might unconscious bias have played a part in how the student nurse responded?

5. How might the student nurse have shared local and national helpline details with Sabina had she stayed? If giving a leaflet, consider ways in which this could potentially increase the risk to Sabina and the child.

6. If Sabina had capacity and did not have children, would this have changed the outcome? Thinking about an adult with capacity making an unwise decision and leaving the ED, reflect on what you might do and how that might make you feel.

Further information

VALUES

Empathy Being empathetic in nursing practice is being able to not only understand the feelings of another person but also having the ability to communicate that understanding to the other person. Empathy is vital for the development and maintenance of therapeutic relationships (for further information see McKinnon, 2018).

Competence The Department of Health (2012, p 13) describes competence as incorporating '*the ability to understand an individual's health and social needs and the expertise, clinical and technical knowledge to deliver effective care and treatments based on research and evidence*'.

Courage According to the 6Cs (Department of Health, 2012, p 13): '*Courage enables us to do the right thing for the people we care for, to speak up when we have concerns and to have the personal strength and vision to innovate and to embrace new ways of working*'.

Professionalism The NMC (2018b) describe professionalism as being characterised by '*autonomous evidence-based decision making by members of an occupation who share the same values and education*', expressing the understanding that in nursing this leads to '*the consistent provision of safe, effective, person-centred outcomes that support people and their families and carers, to achieve an optimal status of health and well-being*'.

Raising concerns The NHS Constitution expects all NHS staff to raise concerns (Department of Health & Social Care, 2021), and it is a professional requirement for nurses to raise safeguarding concerns about people who may be at risk (NMC, 2018b).

Assumptions Making premature judgements and assumptions can impact the decision-making process in nursing, affecting future actions and care planning in detrimental ways (Nibbelink and Brewer, 2018).

Duty of care to safeguard Nurses have a duty to safeguard all patients, but they must also provide additional measures for patients who are less able to protect themselves from harm or abuse (CQC, 2015). The Nursing and Midwifery Council (NMC, 2018b, p 18) state that nurses must raise concerns immediately if they believe a person is vulnerable or at risk and needs extra support and protection by taking all reasonable steps to protect that person, share information and meet legal requirements.

Communication skills As the foundation of the nurse–patient relationship, these are vital in building trust and compassion in nursing care (Dithole et al, 2017). The NMC (2018b) highlight effective communication as one of the most important professional and ethical nursing characteristics. It promotes high-quality nursing care, positive patient outcomes and the patient's and nurse's satisfaction of care.

Record keeping Accurate record keeping is both a legal requirement and a standard of best practice. The NMC (2018b) set out in Part 10 of the Professional Standards of practice and behaviour for nurses, midwives and nursing associates that clear and effective records must be kept. In cases of domestic abuse, this also requires up-to-date, good-quality, relevant records about children and families to help gain a fuller understanding of the family environment (NSPCC, 2020).

THEORIES

Controlling behaviour A spectrum of acts designed to subordinate a person and/or make them dependent '*by isolating them from sources of support, exploiting their resources and capacities for personal gain, depriving them of the means needed for independence, resistance and escape and regulating their everyday behaviour*' (Home Office, 2015, p 3).

Domestic abuse *'Any incident or pattern of incidents of controlling, coercive, threatening behaviour, violence or abuse between those aged 16 or over who are, or have been, intimate partners or family members regardless of gender or sexuality. The abuse can encompass, but is not limited to psychological, physical, sexual, financial, emotional'* (Home Office, 2022).

Coercive control An act, or a pattern of behaviour, intended to exploit, control, dominate and create dependency where assault, threats, humiliation and intimidation are used to harm, punish or frighten their victim (Home Office, 2015). *'Not only is coercive control the most common context in which [women] are abused, it is also the most dangerous'* (Stark, 2007, p 228).

Cycle of repeated abuse The cycle of abuse is a four-stage cycle used to describe the way abuse sometimes occurs in relationships. The stages – tension, incident, reconciliation and calm – repeat themselves over and over again (Coy and Kelly, 2011).

Child protection The process of protecting individual children identified as having suffered, or who are at risk of, significant harm as a result of abuse or neglect.

Emotional abuse *'The persistent emotional maltreatment of a child such as to cause severe and persistent adverse effects on the child's emotional development. It may involve... seeing or hearing the ill-treatment of another... Some level of emotional abuse is involved in all types of maltreatment of a child, though it may occur alone'* (Department for Education, 2018a, p 107).

Consent Giving permission or agreement for something to happen. There are important medical and legal reasons why health records are kept and, wherever possible, nurses should be open and honest with the individual from the outset as to why, what, how and with whom their information will be shared. However, sometimes it is not appropriate to seek consent, because the individual is unable to give consent, because it is not reasonable to obtain consent or because gaining consent would put a child or young person's safety or well-being at risk.

Information sharing An inherent part of any nurse's role. Decisions about what and how much information to share, with whom and when, can affect a person's life by ensuring they receive the right services at the right time and can prevent a need from worsening. For more information on the seven golden rules to sharing information, see Department for Education (2018b).

Vulnerability The term vulnerable is often used to mean in need of protection. In Part 3.4 of the Code (NMC, 2018b), it states that nurses should *'act as an advocate for the vulnerable, challenging poor practice and discriminatory attitudes and behaviour relating to their care'*. The Department of Health (2011) states that a person's vulnerability is influenced by three key factors: their resilience (such as their support networks, personal strengths and coping mechanisms), personal circumstances (such as age – the very young and old can be more vulnerable, health status or disability) and environmental risks (such as social contact, isolation, what care and services they can access, their community facilities). Additional 'vulnerability factors' for some people mean that they may sometimes need to be safeguarded by professionals, but nurses should not assume that, just because a person has an illness or a disability, they are necessarily at risk of harm.

Open questions An open-ended question is a question that cannot be answered with a simple 'yes' or 'no' response, or with a fixed response. Open-ended questions are phrased to elicit a longer response.

APPROACHES

Recognising signs of abuse Signs of abuse can often be difficult to detect as abuse can range from physical abuse, domestic violence, sexual abuse, psychological abuse, financial abuse, modern slavery, discriminatory abuse, organizational abuse, neglect of acts and self-neglect. The SCIE (2020) website provides useful information to help practitioners identify abuse and recognise indicators.

De-escalation The use of techniques including verbal and non-verbal communication skills aimed at defusing anger and stopping aggression (NICE, 2015). It is an approach for early recognition of anger and aggression and managing violent behaviour in a calm and compassionate manner.

Multi-agency working Vital to effective safeguarding (Sidebotham et al, 2016). It is when professionals from various agencies work together to share information, assess risk, find safeguarding solutions or provide support for those who have been affected by issues such as abuse or neglect. For more information, read HM Government (2018) *Working Together to Safeguard Children*.

Paramountcy The Children Act 1989 sets out the obligation to put the welfare of the child first, so that any actions must be in the best interests of the child. This principle of 'paramountcy' means that the child's rights should take priority over the rights and wishes of parents.

MODELS

Duluth wheel of power and control The Duluth wheel (Duluth Model, 2022) makes visible common abusive behaviours or tactics used in an abusive relationship by identifying the patterns, intentions and impact of domestic abuse.

Safeguarding clinical supervision Safeguarding is complex and challenging. Therefore, nurses should have access to regular and protected supervision with an experienced and trained supervisor (Smikle, 2018) so that they can reflect on their decision making and actions taken, as well as potential strategies for future practice.

7 Golden Rules of Information Sharing Legally, information must be shared when a child is at risk of harm. However, being certain about whether and what to share can be worrying. The 7 Golden Rules of Information Sharing (Department of Education, 2018b) is a framework for making decisions about sharing personal information on a case-by-case basis. For more information, see HM Government (Department for Education, 2018b): information sharing advice for practitioners providing safeguarding services to children.

Further reading

Dheensa S and Feder G (2022) Sharing Information about Domestic Violence and Abuse in Healthcare: An Analysis of English Guidance and Recommendations for Good Practice. *British Medical Journal*, 2022(12): e057022.

Griffith, R and Tengnah, C (2020) *Law and Professional Issues in Nursing*. 5th ed. London: Learning Matters.

Keeling, J and Goosey, D (2020) *Safeguarding Across the Lifespan*. London: Sage. (Chapter 11 discusses safeguarding issues around domestic abuse.)

HM Governmemt (2018) *Working Together to Safeguard Children: A Guide to Inter-agency Working to Safeguard and Promote the Welfare of Children*. [online] Available at: https://assets.publishing.service.gov.uk/government/uploads/system/uploads/attachment_data/file/942454/Working_together_to_safeguard_children_inter_agency_guidance.pdf (accessed 13 January 2023).

HM Government (2018) Information Sharing Advice Safeguarding Practitioners. [online] Available at: https://assets.publishing.service.gov.uk/government/uploads/system/uploads/attachment_data/file/1062969/Information_sharing_advice_practitioners_safeguarding_services.pdf (accessed 23 February 2023).

Case study 4
Vanessa: coercion, control and personal choice

Sarah Housden

Vanessa, aged 26, was admitted to our acute medical ward with a kidney infection. This had become serious due to a delay in treatment resulting from her not seeking medical help at an earlier stage. Vanessa presented as a quiet and undemanding person, rarely interacting with nurses or other patients. She was keen to leave hospital as soon as possible, and on the morning after her admission she asked me when I think she will be able to leave. There is nothing unusual in such a question, other than, perhaps, the urgency with which Vanessa asked it, and the anxious look on her face when I said that it will be up to the doctors. She was not keen to wait and see what they had to say during the ward round.

Vanessa was noticeably distressed when advised that she needed to stay in hospital for at least another day or two and that she was not well enough to be discharged. I decided to try to spend some time with her later in the shift to better understand and support her with her anxieties. Many people are fearful of being in hospital, and the majority are keen to get home to more comfortable and familiar surroundings, but there is something about Vanessa which made me think there was more to her anxiety than wanting to be at home.

APPROACH: observational assessment

MODEL: person-centred nursing

APPROACH: intuition

Before I could find time to talk with Vanessa that afternoon, she received a visit from two middle-aged men. I noticed them as they arrived on the ward as they were smartly dressed in dark suits, wearing neatly ironed white shirts, each with a waistcoat and plain, dark tie, suggestive of attending a formal occasion. I was not at the reception desk when they came in, but from where I was standing I could see towards the ward entrance as well as having a clear view of the bay where Vanessa was sleeping.

The nurse who showed the two men to Vanessa's bed gently touched her shoulder, saying that she had some visitors. Neither I nor that nurse could have missed the way the colour drained from Vanessa's face as she opened her eyes and saw who was there.

'*Is everything alright?*' I asked as I passed the bay a few minutes later.

'*Yes, everything's fine, thank you*', came Vanessa's swift reply.

'*Just let me know if you need anything, won't you?*' I said smiling, then turning to the visitors commented that Vanessa was tired and may not want too long a visit. There was no need for me to say this, but somehow I felt protective towards her and was mindful that visits from such formally dressed people might be something Vanessa wanted to be free from while she was unwell and in hospital. They had the look of old-fashioned detectives or a type of debt collector.

At the nurses' station I caught up with my colleague who had shown the visitors in.

'*Did you think there was something odd about those men?*' I queried.

'*Not especially*', she answered, '*at least, not until Vanessa opened her eyes and saw them there! I wanted to ask what the matter was, but of course couldn't with them standing right there*'.

'*Do you think we should report it?*' I asked.

'*Report what? Visiting a patient in hospital isn't a crime you know!*'

'*I suppose not; it's just that something doesn't feel right*', I said, feeling embarrassed about my suspiciousness and beginning to berate myself for jumping to conclusions – especially when I was not even sure what those conclusions were. Something just did not feel right.

Vanessa stayed in hospital a further two days and was visited by the same two men, dressed in the same formal way, each afternoon, with a repeat visit during the evening. After they left each time, Vanessa would become upset and say that she needed to discharge herself. It took time and lots of reassurance that getting better was a slow process and could not be rushed, alongside explanations about the damage that could occur if she did not have enough intravenous antibiotics to get the infection under control before being discharged.

On the second evening after the visitors left, I noticed Vanessa had seemed to turn into herself, so, with many of my tasks accomplished in good time for that shift, it seemed a good idea to spend some time trying to better understand her situation and concerns.

VALUE: empathy

'*I see you had visitors again this evening*', I said, approaching Vanessa. Her back was turned to me, but I could see that she was crying and had half-swallowed the corner of her pillow in an attempt to stifle her sobs. Immediately, Vanessa removed the pillow from her face, and turning towards me, still sobbing, cried out: '*God is so angry with me for being in hospital. I should never have come here. I should have let nature take its course. Asking for treatment was wrong*'.

THEORY: shame

I pulled up a chair next to the bed and, placing my hand gently on her forearm, told Vanessa that I was there to help her in any way I could, and that she was welcome to use me as a listening ear. The truth is that I was a bit perplexed by what she had said. I had not considered that Vanessa might be religious, and that it might be spiritual concerns that were playing on her mind.

MODEL: active listening

APPROACH: non-judgemental approaches; positive regard

That evening, I stayed after the end of my shift, giving her time to talk, asking about her beliefs and the reasons for her concerns about being in hospital. The beliefs she told me about seem fairly mainstream, and not especially surprising. I have come across people from many different cultural, religious and philosophical backgrounds in my work on the ward, and concerns about some medical treatments are not uncommon. I aim to be open-minded; in caring for all kinds of people in nursing, it is essential that assumptions are not made about how individuals from different backgrounds might feel about being unwell, being in hospital and needing treatment. The Western biomedical model of curing ill health upon which much of our health system is based is not a perspective automatically shared by everyone.

VALUE: commitment

MODEL: culturally informed practice

THEORY: health beliefs

APPROACH: open-minded practice

MODEL: biomedicine

As I was leaving that evening, I asked Vanessa what I had been wanting to know since first seeing her smartly dressed visitors: '*Who are the two men who have been visiting, Vanessa? Are they friends, family or…*'

THEORY: alternative perspectives

APPROACH curiosity

I am not sure what my '*or…*' would have consisted of, but Vanessa filled in the gap for me as I hesitated. '*They're the leaders of a faith group I belong to*', she said.

'*Oh, I see*', I answered, and growing bolder in my curiosity asked: '*And do you like them visiting you, Vanessa? Do you want* them to come, or is there someone else you would prefer to see while you're in hospital? Do you have any family or friends apart from those in the faith group, for instance?'

THEORY: making assumptions

Although Vanessa did not answer me straight away, I was sure that this could be a key question which would help her to explore sources of support in addition to the group and its leaders.

MODEL: person-focused communication

I found more time to speak with Vanessa the next evening, when, after her two visitors had gone, she asked me whether I had time for a chat. *'I've been thinking'*, she said, *'about what you asked last night. I do have family, a sister and two brothers, but I haven't spoken to them for some time. They weren't good for me, so I stopped contacting them, changed my phone number, and didn't let them know when I moved two years ago.'*

APPROACHES: respect; non-directive nursing practice

'I see', I answered, not wanting to prejudge the situation or lead the conversation down any particular path. *'How have things been since then?'*

'Well', she hesitated, and lowered her gaze. *'Uncle John and Brother Stephen, they were so kind to me when I first met them.'*

'They're your visitors, are they?' I clarified.

'Yes, they set up the fellowship I joined three years ago. They helped me find somewhere to live and helped me move when the time was right to cut the ties with my family. They were so helpful and understanding. In fact, it was them who helped me to see what a bad influence my family was. My family aren't believers you see and had said things about Stephen and John that were so negative – slurs on their characters. They questioned their motives for setting up a religious organisation when there are plenty of others that exist already. Ours is an exclusive group, you see, and only people who are revealed to John and Stephen can join, and they recognised that I had a calling to be part of the group. They have been so good to me and the rent for the accommodation is okay, and they are so kind to me, even now, or at least when I'm able to contribute more financially to their mission work.'

THEORY non-verbal communication

At that point Vanessa turned her gaze further away from me. There seemed to be a curious mix in her of naivety and lack of awareness. The way she turned away told me that she might be feeling some shame about the situation; yet the way she spoke suggested a possibly blinkered way of looking at the group and its leaders.

I wondered whether these men were visiting so often in order to keep an eye on Vanessa, in a way which was neither compassionate nor altruistic. It was hard to put my finger on why this all felt wrong and why alarm bells were ringing, but it seemed to me that the time had come to talk with the hospital safeguarding team about Vanessa and see whether there was anything I could do to help. From what I had heard I suspected that Vanessa might be experiencing undue control of her life or even coercion to make donations for the work of the group, and that her choices and actions might be subject to excessive control by the group's leaders.

THEORY: spiritual abuse

MODEL: principles of safeguarding practice

Being mindful of the guiding principles of safeguarding, I wanted to work in a collaborative way with Vanessa. I therefore asked her how she would feel about me speaking to a colleague about her situation in the group and the visits from John and Stephen. At this point she looked me directly in the face and said: *'I'd really rather you didn't. I shouldn't have said anything. You made me say things I didn't want to say. Please go away now.'*

THEORY: shared decision making

APPROACH: collaborative risk management

VALUE: patient choice

I went off shift feeling sure that I should say something to the safeguarding team – to at least talk my concerns over with someone, but apart from her apparent naivety, Vanessa did not appear to be a vulnerable adult, so I was unsure, and decided to do nothing until the next morning.

THEORY: vulnerable adults

When I arrived for my next shift, Vanessa had discharged herself and I heard at handover that her two visitors had come to collect her in the early hours of the morning.

THEORY: freedom to choose

Reflections

It can be difficult to discern between a genuine adult safeguarding concern and situations which, while they may be out of the ordinary or beyond my previous experience and therefore challenging for me to process emotionally and intellectually, do not represent a situation which requires a safeguarding referral. Within this scenario, I was unsure whether there was really any need for me to be concerned, and equally uncertain about exactly what it was about Vanessa and her visitors that made me feel uneasy.

These difficulties were exacerbated by not wanting to make assumptions about someone whose experience of religion and expression of faith differed from my own, yet at the same time finding myself with suspicions for which I really had no evidence.

A further influence on my decision making in this situation was that Vanessa would not ordinarily be identified, to the best of my knowledge, as a vulnerable adult as she does not, as far as we know, have ongoing care and support needs. In addition, while mention is made of suspicions of Vanessa's visitors having undue control over her, which may be indicative of some level of spiritual abuse, it is equally possible that she is aware of the manipulative nature of this but chooses to stay in the situation because she benefits from it in some way. Similarly, Section 76 of the Serious Crime Act 2015, which made coercion and control an offence, only applies in the context of domestic abuse where the individual is a family member, or where they are in, or have been in, an intimate relationship with the abuser.

Thus, the dilemmas raised within this scenario cannot easily be resolved, as adults are free to choose to associate with whoever they like, within the bounds of the law, and as much as I may have felt uneasy around the two visitors, any judgement I have made is purely subjective and based on my own life experience and my resulting perspectives on, and understandings of, new religious movements.

Regardless of all the above, the correct action to have taken in the light of my suspicions that something was not quite right would have been to speak to the safeguarding team, if only to clarify the objective information I had, and where this was becoming merged with subjectivity and an emotional response.

It would still be important to do so, after Vanessa has left the ward, for two reasons: first, this helps in generating better understanding of the need for potential safeguarding interventions; and second, in order to ensure that people with the appropriate expertise in this area of practice can follow up with support for Vanessa if this is considered necessary. It is important not to underestimate the role that small pieces of information can play in contributing to a bigger picture, potentially revealing a network of abuse in which vulnerable adults or children may be caught up.

Questions for reflection and discussion

1. Explain and justify actions you would have taken in this scenario if you had been the nurse who connected with Vanessa during her admission.

2. Identify and explore ways in which your personal background and life experiences may influence the way in which you perceive what is normal and lead to judgements about the lives of patients in your care.

3. What role do you consider a nurse has in supporting patients to make choices, even where their perspective on the best choice may differ from that of their patients?

4. In the case of Vanessa, what are the arguments for and against discussing your observations and feelings with the safeguarding and chaplaincy teams at the hospital?

5. Why, and in what ways, is it helpful to have opportunities to explore and discuss potential safeguarding and similar concerns within the workplace?

6. How could you further develop your understanding and awareness of potential safeguarding issues within and beyond religions or cultures which differ from your own?

Further information

VALUES

Care The Code (NMC, 2018b) states that nursing care should be patient centred and provides guidance on 'caring with confidence'.

Compassion Defined in *Compassion in Practice* as '*how care is given through relationships based on empathy, respect and dignity*' (Department of Health, 2012, p 13).

Empathy In nursing practice, empathy is the ability to put yourself in the patient's shoes and understand the world from their perspective. (For further information, see Moudatsou et al, 2020.)

Commitment *Compassion in Practice* states the '*need to build on our commitment to improve the care and experience of our patients*' (Department of Health, 2012, p 13).

Patient choice For consent to treatment or refusal of treatment to be valid in law, the person's decision must be voluntary (they are not unduly influenced or coerced by another person), and they must be appropriately informed of the likely consequences of consenting to, or refusing, that treatment.

THEORIES

Stereotyping Involves using over-generalised beliefs about particular groups of people. These beliefs are likely to be based on assumptions being made about specific characteristics being common to all individuals in the group, for example that they dress similarly, behave in the same way or have shared beliefs about and approaches to life.

Shame An important emotional experience to consider in healthcare because it can lead to treatment avoidance, and therefore to negative health outcomes.

Health beliefs These beliefs, alongside beliefs about the merits or acceptability of specific approaches to healthcare, can be strongly influenced by the social, cultural, religious, ethnic and economic backgrounds of individuals and groups with which those individuals identify.

Alternative perspectives Recognise and incorporate an understanding of everyday reality in which each person, in any situation, is seen as having a unique perspective, thus recognising that objective truth for events has limits and that no one individual can claim to see or recall the situation precisely as it is experienced by others.

Making assumptions Stenhouse (2021, p 27) states that *'nurses must treat people as individuals, avoid making assumptions about them, recognise diversity and individual choice, and respect and uphold their dignity and human rights'.*

Non-verbal communication Involves communicating without speaking, through such things as facial expression, hand gestures, eye contact, touch and body language.

Spiritual abuse Similar to emotional abuse because emotions are part of a person's spirituality. Spiritual abuse includes taking advantage of vulnerable and impressionable people who may be looking for spiritual guidance or acceptance into a religious or faith-based group. Spiritual abuse can potentially occur in any religion or religious denomination.

Shared decision making A co-operative process that involves collaborative communication between medical staff and patients as part of the process of making treatment decisions (see Tracy, 2013, for further information on shared decision making in nursing).

Vulnerable adults Identified as people aged 16 or over who have care needs and whose ability to protect themselves from abuse or neglect is impaired because of a physical/mental disability/illness, or due to old age, for example.

Freedom to choose An adult with mental capacity is free to choose to do whatever they want to, within the law and without doing harm to others. Similarly, it is also permissible for someone assessed as lacking capacity in some situations under the provision of the Mental Capacity Act 2005 to act in a way which other people consider unwise, if they have capacity to make that specific decision at that point in time.

APPROACHES

Observational assessment Can be carried out with or without validated tools, some of which consist of a straightforward checklist of, for example, actions, behaviours, activities and environmental features to look out for. Checklists for observations tend to be either strengths based or deficit based.

Intuition In nursing practice, intuition can play a key role in the professional decision making of experienced practitioners (see Melin-Johansson et al, 2017 for further information).

Advocacy In nursing, advocacy is a process through which it is ensured that every patient is heard and understood. It is an important concept in nursing practice, sometimes used to describe the nurse–patient relationship.

Information and education In healthcare contexts provision consists of opportunities for patients to learn and involves their developing understanding and knowledge aimed at leading to health improvements.

Non-judgemental approaches Such approaches within nursing practice are central to helping practitioners to avoid making premature judgements or assumptions which could impact professional decision making, and so affect future actions and care planning in detrimental ways (Nibbelink and Brewer, 2018).

Positive regard A key aspect of person-centred theory as proposed and practised by Carl Rogers (in Suhd, 1995), enables service users to feel respected and valued within the therapeutic relationship (see Chapman, 2017 for further information on utilising person-centred care in contemporary nursing practice).

Open-minded practice In nursing, open-minded practice encourages practitioners to avoid using stereotypes and making premature judgements or assumptions about the backgrounds, beliefs, cultures and capabilities of patients.

Curiosity Involves going beyond the immediately obvious by observing, listening, asking questions and reflecting on the information you gather. By going beyond superficial and initial sources of information and not accepting everything at face value, practitioners are able to test out any assumptions they may have made about patients, their families and the situations in which they live.

Respect Involves recognising and acknowledging the unconditional value of all people in a way which enables them to maintain their dignity and self-respect.

Non-directive nursing practice Means that nurses, rather than choosing and determining the direction of interventions or care planning, work with patients and other health practitioners to jointly agree the approach to be taken.

Collaborative risk management Involves working alongside patients, and those close to them, to collectively find ways of promoting the individual's well-being, while managing and minimising risk.

MODELS

Person-centred nursing Requires a therapeutic relationship between the nurse and patient that is built on strong communication, and has patients' needs, values and choices central to the development of care delivery (Gluyas, 2015).

Active listening This is an essential aspect of respecting the patients with whom nurses interact. Becoming an effective listener involves actively engaging with people to make sense of what is seen in their body language, in combination with what is heard. Nurses need to hear, consider and process what is said, and this can never be a passive process (Ali, 2018).

Culturally informed practice Recognises and acknowledges the part played by culture in the lives of individuals and the communities in which they live – including those of nurses. Adopting this approach has the potential to improve patient engagement, treatment adherence and health outcomes, as well as staff wellness, as factors core to individual and group identity are given a central place in person-centred care planning and treatments.

Biomedicine The main model used in Western healthcare. As a reductionist approach, it suggests that all illnesses and diseases have specific causes, and that in the presence of such diseases or illnesses specific interventions can be applied in a fairly systematic way to provide relief and a cure.

Person-focused communication Takes into consideration the unique characteristics, communication style and preferences of the individual, as well as working in a way which puts their needs first.

Principles of safeguarding practice There are six principles of safeguarding practice in line with the Care Act 2014. These are: prevention, empowerment, proportional response, protection of the vulnerable, collaboration and accountability.

Further reading

Home Office (2015) *Statutory Guidance Framework: Controlling or Coercive Behaviour in an Intimate or Family Relationship.* [online] Available at: https://assets.publishing.service.gov.uk/government/uploads/system/uploads/attachment_data/file/482528/Controlling_or_coercive_behaviour_-_statutory_guidance.pdf (accessed 23 February 2023).

Laycock, J (2022) *New Religious Movements: The Basics.* Abingdon: Routledge.

Northway, R and Jenkins, R (2013) *Safeguarding Adults in Nursing Practice.* London: Sage.

Oakley, L and Kinmond, K (2013) *Breaking the Silence on Spiritual Abuse.* London: Palgrave Macmillan.

Starns, B (2019) *Safeguarding Adults Together under the Care Act 2014: A Multi-agency Practice Guide.* St Albans: Critical Publishing.

Case study 5
Martin: do no harm

Rebekah Hill

First appointment

I first met Martin over the telephone following his agreement to take part in a research study I was conducting for my doctoral studies. This research study involved interviewing a range of people with a medically confirmed diagnosis of hepatitis C. As a qualitative methods researcher, I was involved in the data collection from study participants over several weeks. Martin's consultant had chatted with him about the research study, and he had agreed to take part, just leaving me to contact him and make the arrangements to meet up.

APPROACH: ethical research

Before I rang Martin, I had a quick review of his details to make sure I fully understood his medical history and current situation. I gleaned that Martin was a 56-year-old male who had been diagnosed with hepatitis C 15 years ago. Martin had received medical treatment to eradicate the virus, but had not responded to it, so he remained hepatitis C positive. Martin was a keen florist and artist; he lived with his wife and had a circle of friends whom he spent time with at weekends. Martin had only a few symptoms of liver disease and was under medical surveillance as an outpatient by his hepatology consultant but had remained well overall.

I inspected the consent form, checking that Martin had agreed to take part in my research study, which was exploring the experiences of living with hepatitis C. The study was being conducted in an attempt to understand what it was like for people living with the condition for whom treatment had been unsuccessful. At the time of this study, this constituted a substantial proportion of those with hepatitis C; since then, thankfully, treatments have improved, with most people with hepatitis C now cured following antiviral treatment (NHS, 2022a).

APPROACH: informed consent

As a research nurse I knew that hepatitis C was an inflammatory disease of the liver caused by the hepatitis C virus triggering both acute and chronic hepatitis, which could range from mild to severe illness. It is usually lifelong, sometimes progressing to liver cirrhosis or cancer (World Health Organization (WHO), 2017). How the disease progress varies from one person to another; how the symptoms are experienced, and the damage done to the liver will also differ from person to person (British Liver Trust (BLT), 2022). Hepatitis C is currently treated using antiviral tablets, which are effective in more than 90 per cent of people (NHS, 2022a). I also knew that for most people with hepatitis C, there is a delay between transmission and diagnosis, since most people (approximately 80 per cent) do not exhibit symptoms (WHO, 2022). New infections are usually asymptomatic; thus, few people are diagnosed when the infection is recent, and as such, most people (around 80 per cent) go onto develop chronic hepatitis C infection, only diagnosed decades after the infection, when symptoms develop secondary to chronic liver damage (WHO, 2022).

After satisfying myself that consent had been given, I telephoned Martin at home to make arrangements for the research interview, hoping to agree on a date and time to meet. The phone was answered by a female: *'Good morning, may I speak to Martin please?'* I blurted out. *'Who is it?'* the female queried. I told her my first name and she replied, *'Who are you, why do you want to speak to Martin?'* I had not anticipated this level of questioning of me and I could not reveal the purpose of the research, since it would have disclosed Martin's hepatitis C status. *'I'm a researcher from the university'*, I replied. She continued, *'Why do you want to talk to Martin then, what's your research about?'* Having not anticipated anyone other than Martin would answer the phone, it came to me immediately that I should have agreed a pseudonym for contact with all the research participants, such as being *'Debbie from the Halifax'*; posing as a cold caller might not have aroused suspicion. I did not really answer her questions, but just repeated that I was a researcher from the university and that the matter was private. I asked if Martin was there again and, fortunately, he came to the phone. Martin and I managed to decide a date and venue for his interview for a couple of weeks' time.

VALUE: effective communication

VALUE: confidentiality

Reflections

I had not expected the first contact to create such a predicament even before the first interview. Although I was not anticipating anyone other than Martin to answer the phone, I really should have. I also should have engaged with the 'Hello, my name is', which may have satisfied Martin's wife, who was clearly curious about who I was and what I wanted. Equally, I should have agreed terms of engagement, such as considering an agreed contact title for the telephone calls which might have been included in the study information given to all potential participants by the consultant. I should have used the seven Cs of communication to have been more effective:

1. *completeness – the communication should be complete;*
2. *conciseness – convey the meaning in the least possible words;*
3. *consideration – step into the shoes of others, take the recipient into consideration;*
4. *clarity – make the message clear and exact;*
5. *concreteness – being clear so the message cannot be misinterpreted;*
6. *courtesy – polite and respectful;*
7. *correctness – no errors in communication.*

(Cutlip and Center, 2005)

This model would have better enabled the purpose of my telephone call to be clear to Martin's wife.

It also occurred to me that, for a moment, I felt vulnerable when arranging a research interview, since it is the participant's choice as to where we met and when, often meaning I am alone in a department with a participant. However, I was grateful to have the security of the university's 'Lone Researcher' policy, whereby I had to notify my supervisor of my whereabouts while data collecting.

MODEL: ethical research

Second appointment

I met Martin in a room at the local university; this had been his preferred choice of venue. It was a cold winter's morning, and we were both dressed informally – I greeted Martin with a handshake and thanked him for attending. We engaged in some small talk, discussing the weather, Martin's journey in and his safe parking, before I asked Martin if it was alright to start the interview, to which he agreed.

VALUE: professionalism

APPROACH: building relationships and trust

'So Martin, please can you tell me what it is like for you to live with hepatitis C?' I asked. Martin started talking immediately: *'Let's start at the beginning'*, he looked away briefly, seemed to take a deep breath and then returned my gaze, *'I got it through drugs*

I guess; it must have been how I got it'. Martin explained how he felt an *'inevitability'* about getting hepatitis C, since he knew many of his friends had also been diagnosed with it. Martin said he had been told his diagnosis in an *'off-hand'* way by a doctor, who casually mentioned finding hepatitis C on a recent blood test. Martin explained openly his previous intravenous drug use and his *'old life'* of drug addiction. *'I never thought I'd get this far; I never figured I'd live beyond my twenties, but here I am – still kicking!'* Martin said with a smile.

Two things then struck me: what would I do if Martin revealed he was currently using intravenous drugs when his consultant thought he was not? I had a professional obligation to disclose this as a nurse, but a moral obligation of confidentiality to Martin as a researcher. Second, it had not occurred to me that Martin might not be alarmed by his hepatitis C status, but just be grateful to be alive, having not expected to survive. This made me question the extent to which I was unaware of any judgements I might hold about what it was like to be living with hepatitis C.

VALUES: honesty; confidentiality

THEORY: unconscious bias

'I want to be as healthy as possible now; I've been given like a second chance, never expected that, so I might as well make the most of it', Martin explained as he talked about wanting to live a healthy life, to eat well and stop smoking, and to reduce his alcohol consumption. It is important that people with hepatitis C try to optimise their health to reduce disease progression (Missah et al, 2008). Factors thought to promote the rate of disease progression are alcohol intake, obesity, diabetes, smoking, age at infection (being over 40 years old at the time of infection), duration of infection, co-infection with HIV or hepatitis B, male gender but not the exposure category or genotype (Nash et al, 2009).

'It's not easy you know; I never thought I'd need to know what a vitamin was, let alone how to get one.' Martin seemed a little sad at this point and looked away. As a nurse I wanted to provide some health education, support and advice, but as a researcher, it was beyond my remit. I was aware of the potential for a dual purpose of the research interview: it was not to provide health education or to counsel, but to extract data, to listen and probe, not to act. Such a skill was alien to me.

MODEL: health promotion

APPROACH: ethical research

VALUE: professionalism

Throughout the interview, I was nodding to show understanding, interest and listening. The first time Martin mentioned *'us'*, I discounted it, but then I noticed he continued to make similar references. Martin described his experiences of healthcare, to

APPROACH: active listening

which he replied, *'you know how it is for people like us, we get treated like dirt most of the time'*. I immediately felt uncomfortable, that Martin had assumed I was also hepatitis C positive in my capacity as the researcher. I was concerned that my nodding to Martin's conversation was interpreted as agreement: is this collusion? Do I continue to nod? Do I also reveal my hepatitis C status? In the moment I thought it best to carry on as the interview was well under way; I neither confirmed nor denied my hepatitis C positive status.

THEORY: stigma

APPROACH: active listening

VALUE: confidentiality

During the interview, Martin made several disparaging comments about nurses. *'You know how they get, bossy nurses, just "yes men" to the consultants'*, he stated as he described a member of nursing staff. Martin explained that his experiences of nurses had not been great, and he talked freely about this. *'Nah, nurses, I don't rate them, little bossy boots'*, Martin continued. I felt uncomfortable that I had not disclosed my professional identity to Martin during the research interview. I had not thought it relevant since my position was that of a researcher, deeming my professional status irrelevant. In retrospect, this was naive. The researcher position is always relevant, whether it be gender, age or professional status; it all impacts on what is said. Had Martin realised I was a nurse, would he have made the derogatory comments about the nursing staff? I do not know the answer, but I know I felt uncomfortable that I had not stated my professional background within the study information.

APPROACH: ethical research

THEORY: bias

VALUE: disclosure

The interview progressed well, and Martin was relaxed, talking freely about different aspects of his life. *'To be honest, I've been lucky; I've never given it to anyone, I've always been careful, even when I've strayed away from home, if you know what I mean'*, he said with a smile. Martin talked about a relationship he'd had previously while still married; he talked about this for some time. *'My missus never found out, thank God.'* Martin explained that his wife had not known about the affair, and they were still married to that day.

I had a dreadful thought: the transcripts from the interview were transcribed, and were due to be returned to Martin's home for him to check. I realised that this might be a problem... what if his wife opened the envelope or read the transcript once opened? The affair might be revealed because of my research – a very unintended consequence. I felt intensely uncomfortable about this. I decided it would be best to not return the transcript, but instead to seek an amendment to my original ethics approval to

VALUE: confidentiality

allow Martin the choice of whether the transcript would be picked up from me or posted to his home.

Lastly, I had given the return of transcripts a great deal of thought; usually it is part of the data collection period (member checking) to allow research participants the opportunity to confirm, tweak or change the data presented. I was concerned about this purpose of transcript return. The transcript was an accurate account of the interview and, as such, could not be changed, because the things in the interview had been said. Returning the transcript to Martin was not intended to be a sharing exercise; for inclusivity, it was just showing him the data he had gifted me. Contentious I know.

Reflections

I feel an assumption was made that I too had hepatitis C when Martin referred to what he supposed were joint experiences. As a researcher, I was concerned that I needed to reveal my hepatitis C status, confidential to me, but I felt privileged to be accepted into the close circle of trusted people with whom the hepatitis C virus was discussed. It was apparent that I was accepted as 'wise' (Goffman, 1963), that is, privy to the secret life of having hepatitis C. On reflection, in future research, I would reveal my professional status; in fact, ethical approval now requires it (UKRI, 2022).

On reflection, two things materialised as important. First, had I misled the participants by not disclosing my professional status; was this professional deceit? Second, had I misrepresented myself as the researcher by omitting to tell the participants I had a healthcare background?

The researcher–healthcare status is a complex situation. Disclosure of professional status risks the interview becoming a therapeutic intervention rather than the intended data collection event. If participants discuss information that one knows to be detrimental to their health, the professional requirement is to disclose, yet the confidentiality assured in the research interview is then breached.

I am conscious that my dual identities of researcher and nurse might create conflict in the research process. Hearing participants talk about their feelings and experiences and seeing their sadness evoked my nursing (or just human) response to make them feel better, to ease their suffering. I felt frustrated at the researcher role in this context.

Participants might be less likely to make disparaging comments about healthcare staff if they are aware the researcher is a professional, and it might later impact on the version of the story told – yet these factors should not influence the extent to which truth is disclosed about the researcher's status.

I did not reveal my nursing status because I was concerned that this information might influence responses during data collection and hence impact on the research process, which transpired to be a valid concern (I understand now that ethical approval processes require that professional status be stated). The debate over researcher versus clinician has been a long-standing dilemma for healthcare professionals, some of whom have questioned the ethics of a research interview that might ignore opportunities to offer therapeutic help. The information sheet and consent forms had purposefully not included my professional identity, just my name. I had felt that this was an important detail since revealing a professional status might have impacted on both the perceived purpose of the interview and what was said within it. I had wanted the participants to talk freely about their experiences of living with hepatitis C. For me, naively, I had argued that my professional status did not need to be disclosed since my status was of no relevance to the interview or had no consequences for the participant taking part in the research.

Third appointment

Having completed the interview in the research study, Martin collected the transcript from me at the university building. He looked pleased to see me and we greeted each other with a smile. We chatted for a while and Martin told me that he had 'changed his outlook' on living with hepatitis C since the interview, and that, in fact, for him it had been therapeutic. Martin explained that 'the interview was the first time I've talked about it, you know, really talked about it, it feels good'. He told me it was the only opportunity he had ever had to discuss having hepatitis C, and that it had stimulated some 'movement' in his acceptance of his hepatitis C status, for the better. 'Talking about it was good for me; it helped me get my head round it all', Martin explained. I felt a twinge of guilt, concerned that Martin had been affected by the interview, but grateful that it had a positive impact.

THEORY: transition

However, I was also worried about the other participants I had interviewed: what if their stories were less encouraging? I had provided access to psychological support, if required, following all interviews. Nonetheless, it is a huge responsibility for a nurse researcher to do no harm. Although we did not meet again, Martin's experience has stayed with me, as has that of all the research participants who gifted me their time and experiences of living with hepatitis C.

APPROACH: ethical research

Reflections

VALUE: non-judgemental care

I realise how deeply self-conscious I was throughout the research process – I am acutely aware of my verbal responses, my facial expressions, every detail of my presence, that I must be perceived to be unbiased and non-judgemental, and that I should not impact on the research data collection or analysis.

APPROACH: active listening

VALUE: effective communication

I am struck by Martin's level of disclosure and trust shown in the interview. Martin talked about a range of deeply personal topics, and I feel overwhelmed by the responsibility of being a healthcare researcher. This responsibility is associated with hearing such personal accounts, keeping the data safe, keeping Martin safe and ensuring there are no negative consequences of participation in the research. Above all else, I must do no harm.

VALUE: confidentiality

Questions for reflection and discussion

1. Do you think you are aware of your own bias? What do you think your bias might be and what steps can you take to minimise the impact?

2. What do you think is the difference between discrimination and stigma? Reflect on why it is important we understand both.

3. Do you think there are occasions when people are labelled or discriminated against in healthcare based on their diagnosis? Why do you think this is?

4. What steps can you take to ensure you do not stigmatise?

5. How do you ensure confidentiality is maintained within your practice?

6. In what ways can you effectively debrief when participating in research data collection?

Further information

VALUES

Effective communication The seven Cs of communication was developed by Cutlip and Center in 1952, and reviewed and published in 2005. In their book *Effective Public Relations*, they suggest we should use the seven Cs to communicate effectively.

Confidentiality Nurses have an obligation to respect and uphold the confidentiality of information shared by patients. The Code of Professional Standards of Practice and Behaviour for Nurses (NMC, 2018b) stipulates that nurses must always respect people's right to privacy and confidentiality.

'Hello, my name is' campaign A campaign to improve healthcare communication. You can find out more about this at: www.hellomynameis.org.uk

Professionalism As nurses, we need to behave in a respectful, trustworthy and proficient manner that will inspire others and role model best practice, acting on and upholding the values of the nursing profession (NMC, 2018b).

Honesty Professional honesty means telling the truth as you know it. Professional integrity is about maintaining ethical behaviour; all healthcare staff must be open and honest with patients (NMC, 2018b).

Disclosure Like honesty, disclosure is the process of making facts or information known to the public to protect them. In the context of this chapter, it is used in relation to transparency of professional status to maintain an honest and trusting relationship.

Non-judgemental care The Code (NMC, 2018b) states that nurses should deliver non-judgemental care which acknowledges all aspects of a patient, from physical to psychological, social, spiritual and cultural. We need to recognise and respect individuality.

THEORIES

Unconscious bias A term used to describe the thoughts and feelings we hold outside our conscious control or awareness, but that might result in us making a judgement or assessment.

Stigma Goffman's theory of stigma (1963) may appear dated, but this seminal work provides the foundation for all social stigma theory. The theory of social stigma proposes that it is an attribute, behaviour or reputation which socially discredits an individual – it causes them to be mentally classified by others as an undesirable, rejected stereotype, rather than as in accordance with a social norm.

Bias The theory of bias involves an inclination or prejudice for or against a person or group, in a way that might be unfair. In contrast, in healthcare research we strive to be impartial, to be unbiased, which is an important consideration for the conduct of ethical research projects (Beauchamp and Childress, 2001).

Transition The theory of transition involves the movement of one state to another, yet transition in the context of this case relates to the process of a changed self-identity and the experience of uncertainty, which exists until a valued identity is achieved (Selder, 1989).

APPROACHES

Ethical research Ethics must be considered throughout the complete cycle of a project. UK Research and Innovation (2022) provide guidance on research ethics and ethical approval must be granted before any research project is started. The following four basic ethical principles must be respected and upheld throughout any research project: autonomy, beneficence, non-maleficence and justice.

Informed consent One of the founding principles of ethical research. For consent to be valid it must be voluntary, informed and the person must have capacity to make the decision. The person must be given all the information about the procedure, the benefits and risks, alternatives and what will happen if consent is not given (Beauchamp and Childress, 2001).

Building relationships and trust Professional therapeutic relationships are built on safe, effective and trusted partnerships in care. It is essential that nurses build therapeutic relationships with patients to optimise care. The Code (NMC, 2018b) has four themes: to prioritise people, practise effectively, preserve safety and promote professionalism and trust, all of which are key to a therapeutic relationship.

Active listening This requires that you listen, understand, respond and reflect on what is being said, and retain the information. Active listening shows patients you are respectful of what they say and helps build trust (Delves-Yates, 2021b).

MODELS

Ethical research This is an approach and a model. The four principles of ethical research of beneficence, non-maleficence, autonomy and justice underpin all approved research studies and must be upheld throughout to protect the public (Beauchamp and Childress, 2001).

Health promotion Nurses have a duty of care to promote health and well-being, prevent ill health and meet changing health and care needs. They play a key role in improving and maintaining mental, physical and behavioural health and well-being of people.

Inclusive research In 2021, the National Institute for Health and Care Research pledged to increase the inclusivity of research, identifying the importance and value of research that is embedded in people and the population and supports public engagement, participation and involvement in research (National Institute for Health and Care Research, 2021).

Further reading

Beauchamp, T and Childress, J (2001) *Principles of Biomedical Ethics*. 5th ed. Oxford: Oxford University Press.

Bowling, A (2005) *Research Methods in Health*. Buckingham: Open University Press.

Health Security Agency (2022) *Hepatitis C in England*. [online] Available at: https://assets.publishing. service.gov.uk/government/uploads/system/uploads/attachment_data/file/1057271/HCV-in-England-2022-full-report.pdf (accessed 23 February 2023).

Kvale, S (2012) *Doing Interviews*. London: Sage Publications.

National Institute for Health and Care Research (2021) Why We Need More Inclusive Research. [online] Available at: https://evidence.nihr.ac.uk/collection/why-we-need-more-inclusive-research (accessed 23 February 2023).

Nursing and Midwifery Council (2018) *The Code: Professional Standards of Practice and Behaviour for Nurses, Midwives and Nursing Associates*. London: NMC.

Part 2

Prioritising care

Case study 6
Molly: cold not dead

Joe Ellis-Gage

I answered the *'red phone'* just as the end of my shift in the emergency department (ED) was approaching. It was ambulance control ringing on behalf of a crew; never a good sign as it means the paramedics and technicians are too busy with the patient to be able to make the pre-alert call themselves.

'Air ambulance inbound. Two-year-old girl. Cardiac arrest post drowning. Cold. Intra-osseous (IO) needle inserted. Active resuscitation under way for 30 minutes. ETA eight minutes.'

I was not meant to be working in resus that shift but as the most experienced paediatric nurse on shift I volunteered to go in. We had eight minutes to prepare for the arrival of this young girl. Paediatric resuscitations often feel hectic with many people involved who are unfamiliar with the set-up of the resus room. I had reflected on my last experience where the room was overwhelmed with well-meaning staff members who did not have a role. I wanted to make sure this one ran as smoothly as possible. I would usually be busy preparing equipment and doing drug calculations but on this day, I delegated that to a colleague, and I stood at the entrance to the resus area. I made everyone sign in so we had an accurate record of who was present and then I started to ask what roles everyone would take. The anaesthetist and operating department practitioner were allocated to the airway, the paediatric registrar was tasked with obtaining intravenous access and two nurses were to rotate with chest compressions. The ED consultant arrived and was happy with my allocation – they were going to lead the arrest. They planned to take a hands-off leadership role in order to have an overview and be free to direct the team; an approach common within emergency departments. Anyone who did not have a role was asked to step back out of the way.

APPROACH: *lighthouse leadership*

I realised there was one role we had not covered – someone to care for the parents. Parents are often present during resuscitation attempts, which can be beneficial for them, but is an additional challenge for the clinical team. Ensuring the parents have a member of staff allocated to stay with them is essential. I looked around to see who was available – the paediatric nurses

THEORY: *witnessed resuscitation*

all had roles allocated to them so could not also care for the parents. I then saw a junior staff nurse, Sam, who was returning from her break. Sam was not a child field nurse but I had seen her work well with relatives before so I asked her if she would be okay to stay with the parents. She was happy to help and said she was relieved to be allocated this role as she would feel out of her depth if she had to assist in the resuscitation itself.

As the resus doors opened, I felt we were as organised as we could be, and we were ready to take over the care of this child. The ambulance crew arrived – four paramedics crowded around the small, lifeless child on the ambulance trolley. As we moved the child across to our trolley one of the crew began a structured handover to us.

APPROACH: ATMIST handover

'This is Molly, she is two years old. Molly fell into a pond which she couldn't get out of. She was fully submerged in the water when her parents found her – we estimate she was in the water for three or four minutes. It took us approximately 15 minutes to get on scene and we had support from the air ambulance. Cardiac arrest on our arrival with some attempts at CPR by her family. Asystole throughout. Adrenaline given via the IO needle in her right leg. Approximately one hour now since she went into the water.'

The crew had done everything they could, but this did not look good. Prolonged resuscitations do not tend to have good outcomes and there was no response from Molly to the attempts so far. We continued with the resuscitation following the national guidelines. As ever during resuscitation attempts, there was a lot of activity around the patient; drugs were administered, attempts were being made to get definitive intravenous access and CPR continued.

MODEL: paediatric advanced life support

Molly felt cold, which was understandable following a drowning and then being exposed during prolonged resuscitation attempts. I took her temperature with a tympanic thermometer, but it came back as 'unrecordable'. At this point I used a rectal probe to try to get an accurate temperature reading – it read 29°C. This was important as hypothermia is a reversible cause of cardiac arrest – we needed to safely normalise the temperature to see if Molly responded before we stopped our resuscitation attempts. European Resuscitation Council guidance suggests that patients should be warmed to a core temperature of 32°C before considering stopping resuscitation attempts (Lott et al, 2021).

APPROACH: ABCDE assessment

I was acutely aware of the presence of Molly's parents. I have always been an advocate for parents being present during resuscitation attempts and had been involved in witnessed resuscitations many times. Although each individual case is unique, when given the proper support families often benefit from witnessing resuscitation attempts (Shaw et al, 2011); however, there are numerous potential disadvantages if implemented poorly (Slater, 2019). I am always conscious of parents being present and I make an extra point of demonstrating the care we are giving to the child; moving them carefully, talking to them if I am about to carry out any sort of intervention and ensuring that colleagues are doing the same. I always think I am not caring for the child differently to if their parents were not there, but I am making a point of the parents seeing the care their child is receiving. I did this with Molly. I wanted the parents to know she was being cared for properly.

VALUE: compassion

I noticed Sam was crouching down next to a chair where Molly's mother was sitting with her head in her hands. I could not see Molly's dad initially but then saw he was pacing up and down outside of the bay. I caught Sam's eye and mouthed '*You okay?*' to her. She gave me a small smile and a nod as she continued to try to comfort both the parents. Shortly after this I saw Sam take both the parents to one of our family rooms nearby – she clearly felt they needed some space away from the resuscitation.

At this point, the clinical team had a frank discussion. The anaesthetist suggested we stop our attempts as Molly had now had approximately an hour and 20 minutes of active resuscitation with no response. The ED consultant disagreed firmly, believing that we could not stop while Molly's temperature was so low. I could see both sides here – the chances of a successful resuscitation at this point were very low so was it really in anyone's best interests to continue our attempts? On the other hand, the guidance is there for a reason and if there was a chance that Molly could survive should we not continue?

THEORY: ethical decision making

I expressed my views to the team – I was keen to be clear and get across my point in what was a tense environment. '*We know that the outcome here is unlikely to be successful, but we owe it to Molly and her family to be sure we have followed the guidance and made every reasonable effort. Then if we are unsuccessful at least they will know we did everything that we could'*.

APPROACH: assertive communication

VALUE: advocacy

Sam returned to the resus bay at this point – she said the parents were having a minute to themselves.

'Do they understand what is happening?' I asked.

'Yes, I've explained about the CPR and what the different equipment is. They understand.'

The team agreed the plan – we would continue for a little longer while we normalised Molly's temperature. We would bring in the parents and explain the plan to them, answer any questions and get their views. For a little while the resuscitation continued with a feeling of relative calm in the room. We had got past the initial hectic initiation of resuscitation, understood our attempts were unlikely to be successful, and were now quietly and calmly continuing with our attempts as we waited for the parents to return. They arrived back after what felt like a lifetime, but it was only around 15 minutes. The ED consultant and I went to speak to the parents at the bottom of the bed.

'It has now been a very long time since Molly's heart stopped. We have been attempting resuscitation for some time and have been doing everything we can. We have given emergency drugs and treatment, but Molly hasn't responded. The reason we have kept going so long is because Molly's temperature was very low and, in these situations, we continue our attempts to resuscitate until that temperature is normal. We are at that point now and as a team we think it is time to stop our treatment.'

'Because her heart is beating for itself?' Molly's dad asked. He did not understand what we were telling him.

'No. I'm afraid Molly's heart isn't going to beat by itself. She can't recover from this, and Molly is going to die.' The use of plain language here is essential – the use of medical jargon or unclear language cannot always be interpreted by the family (Bogle and Go, 2015).

At this point both parents broke down. They began to cry but also to get angry, directing this at me and the consultant.

'Why did you keep going if you couldn't save her?'

'He was talking to her', Molly's dad pointed at me. *'I saw him moving her, so she was comfortable on the bed. You don't talk to dead people.'*

'The other nurse said you were still going because you thought you could save Molly. But you weren't. You were just doing it so you could tick off the list on your guidelines.'

This went on for some time. Both parents were asking question after question. They were cross with us and accused us of giving them false hope. We tried to balance the need to get across the facts of the situation while showing the parents that we had done everything we could and did everything in the best interests of Molly.

'The other nurse kept saying she was in the best hands. If you had tried for a bit and then stopped, I would have understood. But the longer you went on, the more we thought it was because what you were doing was working. We thought she would be okay.'

We stopped the resuscitation soon after. We cared for Molly and supported her parents as best we could, but we had lost their trust. They did not listen to us and wanted to leave as soon as they could. When they left, I could not help thinking we had let them down.

Reflections

Following all resuscitation attempts you are left with *'what if there was something I missed?'* or *'did we really do everything we could?'* questions. This is of course more likely when the patient is a child. However, following this unsuccessful resuscitation attempt it was not the medical management that I was left reflecting on. I was just thinking of the parents and what should have been done differently.

Nobody is ever prepared for a visit to an emergency department but especially not when it is because your child is in cardiac arrest. From the moment these parents arrived, they should have been cared for appropriately by someone who was adequately prepared to do so. Sam was not the right person, and I should never have put her in that position. With hindsight, when Sam expressed relief about not being needed as part of the active resuscitation team, that should have been the time for me to realise that my allocation was not ideal. Sam did not feel confident carrying out the tasks involved with a paediatric resuscitation attempt because she was inexperienced. She had never even witnessed one before. So how could she be expected to support the parents, answer their challenging questions and give a realistic overview of what was happening? Sam did her best and she worked hard to reassure and comfort the parents but that was not all they needed. Families need this compassion but they also need clear information with open and transparent understanding of the potential outcome. This can reduce parental anxiety and even allow them to start to accept the death of their child.

But overall, parents need to trust the team caring for their child. The miscommunication, regardless of how well intentioned, lost us that trust, which led to increased anger and stress. When they look back on that day, I do not think they will remember the large team of people doing everything they could for Molly. I do not think they will remember that we followed the guidance and made sure she had every chance of survival. They will remember confusion, poor communication and a lack of care. We should have supported this family better.

Questions for reflection and discussion

1. What is the best approach when managing parental expectations during paediatric resuscitation?

2. Who should care for the parents during a resuscitation?

3. Is supporting parents during a resuscitation of equal importance to the clinical roles?

4. How much involvement should parents have in decision making during resuscitation attempts and how can they be involved?

5. What do you think might be the impact of witnessed resuscitation on staff members?

6. What type of training do nurses need in order to be better prepared for family-witnessed resuscitation and why?

Further information

VALUES

Compassion Providing care in a supportive, caring and empathetic manner. Seen to be essential to nursing and closely linked to the building of therapeutic relationships (Su et al, 2020).

Advocacy To represent and work in the best interests of a patient or family, aiding them to understand and access appropriate support.

THEORIES

Witnessed resuscitation The presence of family members during active resuscitation attempts. More common within paediatrics but increasingly becoming part of adult resuscitation attempts. Witnessed resuscitation has the potential to be beneficial to families but staff need to be supported and trained to do this to reduce the likelihood of negative responses (Resuscitation Council UK, 2021a).

Ethical decision making The need to make choices about patient care, potentially involving the patient and family, based on the key ethical principles of beneficence, non-maleficence, autonomy and justice. These are rarely simple decisions with a clear answer such as deciding to continue or stop resuscitation attempts.

Non-abandonment Demonstration of the clinician's commitment to provide ongoing care in a patient's best interest, involving them where possible (Quill and Cassel, 1995).

APPROACHES

Lighthouse leadership An approach where the leader guides team members, only rarely needing to get involved in tasks themselves. Commonly used within emergency departments during resuscitation attempts (Cooper and Wakelam, 1999).

ATMIST handover A structured handover tool used by ambulance crews to handover patients to hospital staff. The approach covers Age, Time, Mechanism, Injuries, Signs and Treatment (Lirette et al, 2018).

ABCDE assessment A systematic approach to assessing all deteriorating or critically ill patients (Resuscitation Council UK, 2021b). The patient is assessed in the following order: airway, breathing, circulation, disability and exposure. In this scenario checking the temperature is included during the disability assessment stage.

Assertive communication The ability of a nurse to communicate their views clearly and firmly on a situation. Essential as part of patient advocacy (Sibiya, 2018).

MODELS

Paediatric advanced life support National guidance focusing on the care of acutely unwell children, providing clear guidance during resuscitation (Resuscitation Council UK, 2021b).

Further reading

Dragann, B, Melnychuk, E, Wilson, C, Lambert, R and Maffei, F (2016) Resuscitation of a Pediatric Drowning in Hypothermic Cardiac Arrest. *Air Medical Journal*, 35(2): 86–7.

Ghavi, A, Hassankhani, H, Powers, K, Ashadi-Bostanabad, Namdar-Areshtanab, H and Heiderzadeh, M (2022) Parental Support Needs During Pediatric Resuscitation: A Systematic Review. *International Emergency Nursing*, 63: 1–11.

Grimes, C (2020) The Effects of Family-Witnessed Resuscitation on Health Professionals. *British Journal of Nursing*, 29(15): 892–6.

Powell, S (2021) Breaking Bad News to Patients in the Emergency Department. *Emergency Nurse*, 30(2): 32–40.

Powers, K, Duncan, J and Renee Twibell, K (2022) Family Support Person Role During Resuscitation: A Qualitative Exploration. *Journal of Clinical Nursing*, 32: 409–21.

Case study 7
James: to donate or not to donate?

Joe Ellis-Gage

I first knew of James when I received the phone call from Rose, the staff nurse on critical care (CC). She gave me a very brief summary of the situation – *'we have a 21-year-old male, James. Traumatic brain injury. For withdrawal of life-sustaining treatment. Family present'* – and asked me to see him. This was the usual level of detail the specialist nurses in organ donation (SNODs) would receive, usually from a busy nurse asked to make a referral while caring for an acutely unwell patient and their family. At this point I wanted to find out more: When had this happened? Was James requiring any inotropic support? Did he have other signifi-cant injuries? What were his blood results? What was his med-ical history? However, it was clear Rose did not have time to answer me now, so I did not probe further. Fortunately, I was on site in the hospital so I walked down to the CC unit to see if James could be a suitable organ donor.

VALUE: patience

James had been involved in a high-speed road traffic collision – his motorbike had hit the back of a stationary car on a motorway. He had suffered a cerebral haemorrhage and a significant mid-line shift was noted on his CT (computerised tomography) scan. James' brain was impacted by the increased pressure due to the bleed. Significant midline shifts are linked to very increased mor-tality rates (Puffer et al, 2018). Although young adults tended to be suitable for organ donation, there would still be plenty to review – past medical history, social history, travel history, the injuries sustained as part of the crash and the potential impact on James' organs. These reviews were essential to get as full a picture of the person referred as possible. This was of course important to ensure the safety and suitability of the organs to be donated – the role of the SNOD is to gather as much information as possible to ensure transplant surgeons and their patients can make a fully informed decision about whether to accept the offer of an organ. If information is missed or inaccurate it could lead to a donated organ later being deemed unsuitable for transplant-ation or worse still being transplanted inappropriately. However, I feel that the initial review is more important in supporting the family of the potential donor. I always wanted to be fully informed about a situation before meeting a family to discuss the options. Without this information I could be raising the sensitive issue of

APPROACH: patient safety

organ donation, only to later realise the donor would be unsuitable. For families supportive of donation, I was conscious I did not ever want to give them false hope. For families not supportive of donation I did not ever want to raise the issue unnecessarily.

I walked towards the unit and immediately knew there was not going to be time for the usual full assessment before I met the family. There was a large group of people stood around the entrance to CC – I did not need to swipe my badge as they were holding the door open. They knew I was coming and they were waiting for me. I arrived on the unit and Rose greeted me.

'Hi! Thanks for coming so quickly – the family are in here.'

Rose turned and started to walk towards the relatives' room.

'Rose – can I have a quick look at the notes first and maybe see James? Just so I can assess his suitability and can answer the family's questions.'

MODEL: S-P-w-ICE-S

I logged on to a computer and while it was loading, I started to question Rose; I needed to be as prepared as possible before I met the family. The first step in challenging conversations, especially those where you are breaking bad news, is to prepare yourself so you are as aware of the situation as possible and that you have a plan for the conversation (Meitar and Karnieli-Miller, 2022).

'Which family members are here?'

'Mum, dad and little sister', Rose replied, *'and his aunt, uncles, three grandparents, two of his friends…'* The list went on – James was well loved and a lot of people wanted to be with him. In total there were 14 people.

'How much do they understand of the situation?'

'They get it', Rose replied quickly. *'They have seen his CT scan and had it explained by the consultant. They've asked sensible questions and been given clear answers. They know James can't survive.'*

'How are they coping?'

'Better than most. They are upset but accepting. His sister seems to have taken on the role of being in charge. They just keep asking for more time with him.'

We were sitting at a semi-private nurses' station – away from the bedside and the family but still in full view. I could feel we were being watched as the family anxiously paced at the end of the room. They had been told I would come and speak with them so now I was here they did not understand the delay. James' sister came over and spoke to Rose, trying to find out what was happening now.

I wanted to be as prepared as possible before starting the conversation, but the computer was still loading. I made a quick call and confirmed that James was on the Organ Donor Register (ODR). I did not want to leave the family waiting any longer, so I left the loading computer and went to meet them.

The first minutes with a family can be the most important; it is a time to gain their trust, explain your role and most importantly identify their needs. The family were relieved when I spoke with them. They had discussed organ donation with James and he had clearly told them he would want to donate his organs if something were to happen to him. I gave them information on the process and answered their questions; they were happy for us to proceed. I asked to spend some time with just James' parents and his sister. I needed to ask several questions about James' medical, social and travel history. These included personal questions and I was conscious of only asking those who were essential. They were happy to answer and nothing of note came up during the conversation. I explained the next steps were for me to collate all the information I could about James, carry out a physical assessment, review his medical notes and carry out some additional tests, which included sending away some blood tests for a virology test. I explained all of this had to be completed before we could proceed.

APPROACH: effective communication

VALUE: altruism

APPROACH: valid consent

VALUE: confidentiality

This process is not quick; it is not uncommon for there to be 12–24 hours between consent and donation. By now it was around 2am. I was sitting in the sister's office with a cup of coffee, tired but busy making sure I had all the patient assessment information I needed. I was still waiting on the virology results – once these were back, I should be in a position to 'offer'. This was the process of contacting transplant centres around the country to see if they had a suitable recipient for the organs being offered. We were given a list of centres and the order in which to contact them – you had to wait for one centre to answer before you could proceed or contact the next centre to offer to them. This was not a quick process, but we always ensured the organs were 'placed' before we proceeded with organ retrieval.

There was a knock at the door. I turned as deputy charge nurse Leo entered – Rose's shift had finished hours earlier and Leo was now caring for James and his family.

'Can you come through? James is unstable. I think we are going to have to call off the organ donation.'

I walked through to the bedside and saw the family gathered around. James' blood pressure has dropped dramatically. His pulse was rising. It was clear that without intervention he would die very soon. The critical care registrar came over and we stepped away from the family.

'What now?' the registrar asked. *'Are you ready for the retrieval?'*

'No. We haven't got the virology results back yet and we haven't placed the organs.'

'Okay, well it is time to call it off then. He is dying.'

I wasn't happy with this plan. Surely this could not be the end of it. James was on the ODR. His family were so supportive of donation – they saw it as the only positive that could come out of this situation.

'Can we increase his metaraminol infusion? Give him some more fluid? Buy us a bit more time to see if I can arrange the donation?' These treatments were already in place but not at an effective level –increased inotropic support would increase his blood pressure and give me time to consider the next steps.

'It isn't appropriate; we can't justify further interventions on him when he is clearly dying.'

THEORY: medical justice

I wasn't asking for new interventions, just adapting the ones already in place. Was I right to be asking for this or was the registrar right that this was the time to withdraw? Thoughts were rushing through my head.

• Should the donation be called off or should it proceed at pace?

• What would James have wanted?

• What was best for his family?

- What was best for the potential recipients of the donated organs?

- What level of medical intervention was appropriate to maintain adequate perfusion of organs prior to donation?

- Could we justify going ahead with the invasive donation procedure when there was doubt over the suitability of the organs?

- Was it right to continue to use resources within the hospital for a donation that may not be successful?

'I need to speak to the family', I said to the registrar. *'Let me find out how they feel about the situation before we make any final decisions. Will you increase his support while I do that?'*

The registrar reluctantly agreed but set an arbitrary limit on how high he was prepared to increase the inotropic support. I thought about challenging this but could see he was struggling with his own ethical dilemma here – he was uncomfortable with the situation and setting this limit was making him feel a little more in control. I let it go.

We squeezed into the family room with people sitting on the floor, the arms of chairs, the bin. They made space for me to sit on one of the few comfortable chairs – I tried to refuse but they would not have it. I liked this family. They were distraught and did not understand why the donation may not be able to proceed. I told them it was a possibility if we could stabilise James for long enough to get the team of retrieval surgeons here and ready, but I told them I cannot guarantee we would achieve this. James' sister continued in her role as spokesperson for the family.

'Do whatever you need to do so he can donate his organs. He would have wanted this. We want this. Please try.'

I walked back to the bedside, worrying that I was giving them false hope – I had not even spoken to the retrieval surgeons yet. What if the local team were out on a call? We did not have time for anyone further away to drive to us.

Back at the bedside Leo looked calmer than he did before – James had responded well to the increase in support. Maybe we did have time to do this. I made a point of documenting my discussions with the family and the plan to proceed with donation in the patient records.

The next hour flew by. I made some phone calls; theatres have a space available that we can use straight away; the retrieval surgeons are fortunately not out elsewhere and can be in theatre within 45 minutes. I explained the process to the family – we would extubate James and turn off his medication infusions. We will keep him comfortable and expect that he will die very quickly. After this we will rapidly proceed with the organ retrieval. I explained that there are still some unknowns (virology results, organ placing, organ condition and viability). The family needed to understand there was a risk James' organs would be retrieved but not transplanted.

I made one final call to the on-call manager for organ donation. I was phoning to get their approval to go ahead with the donation while still awaiting virology results and without having placed any organs yet. I was apprehensive as if they said no, I would need to call everything off. They were covering the whole country, would likely have been asleep until I rung and would quite likely not know me personally. I needed to make sure I have them all the relevant information clearly and succinctly. My request was unusual, and I expected to be challenged. I was not wrong.

'You are not following the guidance. It is potentially unsafe and may be a waste of time. It isn't fair on the family to proceed. You need to stand down.'

VALUE: advocacy

I took a second to think before I replied. I needed to hold my ground and put across my views on the situation. There is a shortage of organs available for transplantation (Silva et al, 2022), and I was confident these organs would be suitable; it did not feel right to back out now.

'He is on the ODR. He is young, previously fit with no medical history at all. His bloods are all normal. He has no high-risk social or travel history. His organs are highly likely to be suitable for transplant. His family want this to go ahead more than anything. The virology results will be back anytime, and we will have the results before the organs are sent to the transplant centres. I can do the organ offering while we are in theatre – I've made a couple of

APPROACH: assertive communication

calls and transplant surgeons have said they would be interested. I think it is the right thing to do'.

'Okay. Go for it.'

And that was it. We were in theatre before we knew it. James died within a minute of his ventilation being stopped and the organ retrieval went ahead. The virology results came back clear. His liver and kidneys were in near-perfect condition and were accepted by the first centres we offered to. They were successfully transplanted into three grateful recipients the same day. The family were so excited when I told them the organs had been retrieved and were suitable. They cried, they hugged each other, and they were all confident it was the best thing that could have come out of such a sad situation.

Reflections

As I went home that morning, I was pleased. James had saved lives with his donation. I had spent valuable time with his family and supported them through the most difficult night of their life. They had openly thanked me for my time and support. But I did have a nagging doubt in my head – what if his organs hadn't been suitable? What if they had been retrieved but no centre had accepted them, or the virology results had come back with an unexpected result? Would I have been right to push ahead with the donation then?

THEORY: non-maleficence

I had been open and clear with the family from the start. I always made a point of being honest with families early on – they need to know that not all donated organs are able to be transplanted and that sometimes even when they are the recipient does not survive. I was confident that if James' organs had been unsuitable for transplantation, his family would have understood. They may have even been comforted by the fact that we had tried – I can recall another family who were just pleased to have given it a go even though their relative's organs were deemed unsuitable after donation. *'It's what he would have wanted'*, they said. I think James' family may have been the same.

But what about the bigger picture? – the staff, the resources and the money that went into the process. If James' organs had been retrieved and then deemed unsuitable, would I have been able to justify the time and cost to get to that point? Is it better to have tried to save lives while supporting someone's dying wish to donate and fail than to have not tried at all?

Questions for reflection and discussion

1. How can family expectations be managed during an end-of-life and potential organ donation situation?

2. How do you know a family truly comprehends the information you are giving them during times of high stress and emotion?

3. How might you need to adapt your approach if you think a family does not understand the information you are giving?

4. How best can staff be supported when caring for patients and families in these stressful situations?

5. When might the needs and demands of an organisation take priority over the needs of an individual? Explore the circumstances when this might occur.

6. With many patients on the transplant waiting list, do we need to take a more proactive, yet potentially riskier, approach more often to increase donation rates? If so, what might our approach be and why?

Further information

VALUES

Patience The ability to remain calm while waiting for something. Within nursing it is essential in patient interactions and in building relationships with colleagues.

Altruism The act of doing something for others with no clear benefit to yourself. In this case consenting to be on the Organ Donor Register so that organs can be donated to others in need after death.

Confidentiality The importance of maintaining patient privacy. The Nursing and Midwifery Council (2018b) emphasise the importance of respecting privacy even after a patient's death and to share information with families in line with the law.

Empathy The ability to understand how someone else is feeling without passing judgement. An essential nursing attribute.

Openness and transparency Being open and honest with patients, and their families, about their care. Noted by Francis (2013) to be the *'cornerstone of healthcare'* in the Mid Staffordshire NHS Foundation Trust Public Inquiry.

Advocacy To represent and work in the best interests of a patient or family, aiding them to understand and access appropriate support.

THEORIES

Medical justice Ensuring that practice is fair, legal and ethical while making sure no patient or group are disadvantaged.

Distributive justice Within healthcare, distributive justice focuses on fair allocation and prioritisation of resources. A complex issue currently within healthcare with increasing demands and increasing services but linked to a lack of resources (Varkey, 2021).

Non-maleficence Doing no harm. This must be considered in both proceeding with an intervention and in not intervening. It is important to balance the potential benefits of a course of action against the potential harms (Varkey, 2021).

APPROACHES

Patient safety The process of *'maximising the things that go right and minimising the things that go wrong for people experiencing healthcare'* (NHS England and NHS Improvement, 2019, p 6).

Patient and family-centred care Involving patients and their families in the planning of their care to ensure mutually agreeable goals. An approach increasingly favoured in intensive care settings (Mitchell et al, 2016).

Effective communication The exchange of communication between two or more people via a variety of means. This includes verbal communication, non-verbal communication and active listening.

Valid consent Consent that is voluntary, informed and from a patient with capacity (NHS, 2019).

Assertive communication The ability of a nurse to communicate their views clearly and firmly on a situation. Essential as part of patient advocacy (Sibiya, 2018).

MODELS

S-P-w-ICE-S An adapted version of the original SPIKES six-step model used to structure the process of breaking bad news (Meitar and Karnieli-Miller, 2022).

Further reading

Cooper, J (2021) Time, Resourcing, and Ethics: How the Routinisation of Organ Donation after Circulatory Death in the NHS Has Created New Ethical Issues. *Critical Public Health*, 33(2): 174–84.

Gardiner, D, Charlesworth, M, Rubino, A and Madden, S (2020) The Rise of Organ Donation After Circulatory Death: A Narrative Review. *Anaesthesia*, 75(9): 1215–22.

National Institute for Health and Care Excellence (NICE) (2016) *Surveillance Report 2016 – Organ Donation for Transplantation: Improving Donor Identification and Consent Rates for Deceased Organ Donation (2011) NICE Guideline CG135.* London: NICE.

Sarti, A, Sutherland, S, Meade, M, Shemie, S, Landriault, A, Vanderspank-Wright, B, Valiani, S, Keenan, S, Weiss, M, Werestiuk, K, Kramer, A, Kawchuk, J, Beed, S, Dhanani, S, Pagliarello, G, Chassé, M, Lotherington, K, Gatien, M, Parsons, K, Chandler, J, Nickerson, P and Cardinal, P (2022) The Experiences of Family Members of Deceased Organ Donors and Suggestions to Improve the Donation Process: A Qualitative Study. *Canadian Medical Association Journal*, 194(30): 1054–61.

Wu, D and Oniscu, G (2022) Piloting Uncontrolled DCD Organ Donation in the UK; Overview, Lessons and Future Steps. *Current Transplantation Reports*, 9: 250–6.

Case study 8
Aiyana: for crying out loud!

Sarah Housden

Aiyana was born in Bangladesh and has lived in the UK since early childhood. As a health practitioner working on a busy ward, I am informed of her admission during handover one morning where it is said that she has dementia, cannot communicate and constantly shouts for help. Nothing seems to help calm her down and some staff are becoming tired of asking her to be quiet, as are her fellow patients. There is some discontent growing on the ward over the disruptiveness of her vocalisations. She has shown no interest in food or drink, and it seems that there is no way of finding out from her what she usually drinks and eats.

THEORIES: assumptions about communication in dementia; communication of unmet need; stress and distress in dementia

The reality of Aiyana's calling out quickly becomes clear as I hear shouting coming from a bay at the end of the ward furthest away from the staff handover area. It sounds as though more than one person is shouting, and fearing that something is seriously wrong, I immediately head in that direction.

APPROACHES: resolving conflict; need for supported nutrition and hydration

VALUE: caring

As I approach the bay, I can guess which of the six women in the bay is Aiyana as she is lying in bed calling out in a high-pitched voice: '*Help! Nurse, help. Help me! Help! Help! Nurse!*'

THEORY: repetitive vocalisations in dementia

She is not the only one of the women expressing distress, as another lady is shouting in a much deeper, gruffer voice which expresses anger and exasperation alongside distress: '*Can't you shut her up nurse? Can't you move her? Why is she here in this bay? This ward is not meant to be for people like her! Why can't you move her to another ward? There are sick people here and we need to get some peace and quiet!*' Meanwhile, other patient voices chipped in with expressions of frustration and exasperation: '*For goodness' sake!*' and '*Is there any way that you could all shut the goodness up?*'

It is difficult for me to know where best to start to restore calm and reduce the noise levels as swiftly as possible. I go over to the most vocal lady first and say calmly and with confidence: '*Thank you for your concerns; I understand that this makes you feel stressed, and we will do our best to meet the needs of every patient.*' The woman looks at me, and then turns her back on me muttering ill-humouredly as she does so.

VALUE: competence

APPROACH: communication

I really do understand how she feels and can imagine that needing to be in hospital for more than a short while without getting much-needed rest must leave patients with real frustrations. However, I am also quite sure that adding to the noise by shouting back does nothing to restore the peace of the ward.

I cross over to the bed where Aiyana now lies rocking herself in a self-soothing action while also crying with a mournful, wailing sound. The name label at the top of the bed confirms that she is Aiyana. She swiftly quietens and slows the repetitive rocking as I touch her hand and say her name softly: 'Aiyana, hello Aiyana. How are you? I'm here, you're not alone.' As well as the change in her movements, listening carefully I can hear that she is still saying 'Help' but now she is doing so in a soft tone and with what sounds like a note of relief, changing gradually to what sounds like quite a jovial tone as I continue to speak words of reassurance and keep my hand over hers, cupping it gently.

I wonder why Aiyana has been perceived and identified as being unable to communicate. She may have few words left with which to voice her concerns, but it is clear to me that she has been communicating her distress very effectively before I approached her. I imagine how threatening the environment must seem to a person who is unwell, and who, because of the effects of moderately advanced dementia, is unsure of where she is, so feels alone and uncertain of what is happening. Then, to make things worse, every time she cries out for help, being desperately in need of some words of reassurance and comfort, the already alien environment becomes even more threatening as angry-sounding voices (of other patients) are heard shouting back. It is clear too that Aiyana understands a certain amount of communication – the spoken words as well as their tone, as well as the meaning of gentle touch.

I wonder again why Aiyana came to be identified as being non-communicative. This may have been due to lack of understanding of the different ways people living with dementia can communicate through the tone of their vocalisations as well, as with single words which can mean quite different things when said in different tone of voice. The effects of expressive and receptive aphasia on those whose dementia is moving to a more advanced stage can be seriously detrimental to well-being where people do not recognise the need to draw upon a person's remaining skills and abilities, rather than just seeing what they have lost.

I also wonder whether a note in her medical records stating that English is not Aiyana's first language has influenced expectations about her ability to communicate with staff. It might be that assumptions have been made, and that the communication barriers that are being experienced have been created primarily by people around Aiyana, rather than by her own difficulties. It could be that she has not been given sufficient time to process and interpret questions, or to formulate responses to questions now that she needs more time to understand what is said and to give a response. The result? People spending less time attempting to communicate and a label is eventually applied that is not just misleading but is potentially detrimental to Aiyana's well-being and the delivery of appropriate care. Inappropriate approaches to communication from ward staff who have insufficient understanding of how to communicate effectively with people experiencing aphasia for reasons related to dementia and other similar acquired neurological conditions appear to be the central cause of Aiyana's distress, as well as the stress this is causing for those around her.

> THEORY: need for culturally informed practice

> THEORIES: disabling social environment; outpacing; cognitive impairment

> MODEL: malignant social psychology

It is not long, just a minute or two, before my colleague Liz comes along and, peering down at Aiyana, says: *'It's nice that she's quiet now, but she won't stay that way! Anyway, can you come and help me with the IVs?'*

'I have to go for a while now, Aiyana, but I'll come back later and see how you are.'

> APPROACH: positive communication

'I don't know why you speak to her like that', says Liz. When I ask why she says this, I am aghast to hear her response:

'Aiyana isn't English, so she probably doesn't understand, but she has dementia too, so even if she would once have understood, she couldn't now. She can't communicate at all!'

Taking a deep breath, I decide to use this as an opportunity to support my colleague to see things from a different perspective. *'Liz, when you hear Aiyana calling out, why do you think she does that?'*

> APPROACH: modelling best practice

'They just do that when they have dementia, don't they?'

'Not every patient you've ever worked with who had dementia has done that, have they Liz? And what about if you heard someone crying out like that, and they didn't have dementia. How would you react then?'

Liz and I work well together and have known each other for several months, so I am not concerned about how she might respond to me challenging her thinking on this. We are used to reflecting on our healthcare delivery together and there have been occasions when Liz has helped me see things differently too. However, she is quiet for a minute or two, and I begin to wonder whether she understands my point or not. I am relieved when she does speak, and it is clear she has taken on board what I have said.

APPROACH: reflective practice

Later, returning to the ward after taking a short break, I can hear that the shouting in Aiyana's bay has escalated again. I head in that direction, aware that this means that I am putting to one side a number of other important tasks which need doing urgently.

APPROACH: person-focused versus task-focused care

'I've got this, it's alright', says Liz as she enters the bay just ahead of me. I see her head to Aiyana first, using gentle touch and a calm tone of voice to reassure her. She seems to be modelling her interactions on what she saw me do earlier. I think with a smile how important modelling best practice is in encouraging person-centred healthcare practice.

THEORY: recognising the person behind the dementia

Aiyana responds as she had with me earlier, and gradually becomes still and quieter.

'Would you like a drink, Aiyana?' asks Liz, noticing an unopened carton of juice, probably left from breakfast. Watching the expression on Aiyana's face, Liz wonders aloud, and with a slightly playful tone, whether a cup of tea might be more to her liking.

MODEL: positive person work

'Alright, I really have got the hang of this, because that smile tells me that tea is your preferred drink. Am I right there Aiyana? I think we'd better make a note of that in your "This Is Me" document.'

APPROACH: 'This Is Me'

I leave Liz to it, happy to have made what could be a lasting difference to both of their lives today.

Reflections

The dilemmas nurses face in situations such as this include how to manage the responses of other patients, in the context of needing to treat all patients respectfully while protecting patient confidentiality. While it might seem easier to tell other patients that a person making a lot of noise is confused or has dementia, such confidential information about symptoms and diagnosis is not given to us to share.

Also evident within the scenario is the pressure ward staff can be under in terms of completing set tasks for which they have responsibility. At times, person-centred practice can be overtaken by task-orientated care, especially where it may seem easier and more efficient to do something with a clear beginning and end. Beginning to attempt communication with an individual who needs more time to understand what you are saying, or whose starting point is one of distress, or where there is no communication care plan in place, can seem much more onerous a task simply because of the number of unknown elements. Risks associated with task-orientated approaches to service delivery include the outpacing of patients with cognitive impairment or other complex needs. Outpacing can lead, for instance, to assumptions being made about a patient's abilities and dependence levels, where for example time is not taken to support a patient to get dressed, but they are instead passively dressed by a healthcare practitioner. Taking a strengths-based approach helps to reduce outpacing and to ensure that support is provided only with the aspects of a task which the individual cannot complete – rather than with anything that cannot be done in the timescale defined by the supporting health practitioner.

There is also the question of whether to cause potential inconvenience to colleagues by spending the extra time required to properly understand the needs of a patient living with cognitive impairment. Sometimes it can appear best, in the short term, to do what may appear to be the option colleagues expect you to take – which is to get all tasks completed in the time allocated. However, ideally, the best approach is to create a team consensus on who will spend time on different types of tasks, so that a balance is created between paying attention directly to people and tasks. The reality is that making such decisions can lead to challenges for some nurses, who may be perceived as being less hardworking than other team members.

This case scenario also points to the importance of collaborative working across disciplines, such as with speech and language therapists, to ensure that communication plans are swiftly drawn up, shared and implemented. Similarly, freely available tools such as 'This Is Me' (Alzheimer's Society) can be used across wards and departments if a copy is added to the patient notes. These in turn can be developed as more is learnt about how the patient communicates and information is gathered about what they like to eat, drink and communicate about.

Within this scenario, best practice is modelled to and by healthcare colleagues. Where this works well and best practice is both modelled and explained, improvements in care and service delivery are likely to result. However, there is a significant risk that bad practice is equally likely to be modelled. Practitioners therefore need to be vigilant in discussing approaches to practice, together with both the rationale for implementing specific approaches at particular times, and the research evidence or practice guidance which recommends and supports the approach taken. Should an innovative approach to practice appear to bring about better outcomes for patients, then reflection on practice may help in identifying ideas for quality improvement projects or service evaluation.

Questions for reflection and discussion

1. Identify at least six ways in which you have seen patients who are non-verbal in their communication express their needs, preferences or feelings.

2. How can nurses be encouraged to take the time to identify and record non-verbal means of communication with a view to improving person-centred care?

3. Thinking about people with whom you have worked in a healthcare setting, identify ways in which you could have reduced outpacing and adopted a strengths-based approach to enhance care delivery.

4. What sort of assumptions have you seen being made about patients who cannot communicate verbally or who have only a few words with which they can communicate?

5. Thinking about assumptions which are sometimes made about people from different backgrounds in healthcare settings, how could you work to reduce the impact of such stereotyping?

6. What difficulties or benefits might be associated with a number of staff members and relatives adding to personal profiles such as 'This Is Me' at different times, rather than the profile being filled in by one person at the start of the patient's care journey?

Further information

VALUES

Caring Requires nurses to engage in interactions and interventions which focus on the needs of the whole person. Caring also includes making use of an evidence-based approach to providing the right care, in a timely way, at every stage of life. The Code (NMC, 2018b) states that nursing care should be patient centred and provides guidance on *'caring with confidence'*.

Competence *Compassion in Practice* (Department of Health, 2012, p 13) describes competence as incorporating *'the ability to understand an individual's health and social needs and the expertise, clinical and technical knowledge to deliver effective care and treatments based on research and evidence'*.

Empathy In nursing practice, empathy is the ability to put yourself in the patient's shoes and understand the world from their perspective (for further information, see Moudatsou et al, 2020).

Compassion Defined in *Compassion in Practice* as *'how care is given through relationships based on empathy, respect and dignity'* (Department of Health, 2012, p 13).

Curiosity Involves going beyond the immediately obvious by observing, listening, asking questions and reflecting on the information gathered.

THEORIES

Assumptions about communication in dementia Often made based on limited experience of an individual or poor communication strategies. An example is not giving a person with impaired cognition sufficient time to process a question and formulate their answer before moving on to your next question. Whereas in most conversations, people meet each other halfway, in dementia care, the nurse needs to meet the person where they are.

Communication of unmet need This is a way of understanding actions and vocalisations which practitioners may find challenging in busy care environments. Reframing an action or vocalisation as an expression of unmet need, rather than as 'challenging behaviour', will support communication between the nurse and the person living with dementia and facilitate more effective delivery of person-centred dementia care.

Stress and distress in dementia This is a way of understanding an individual's responses and actions within an environment which they may find confusing. Confusion in an unfamiliar environment can be caused by the décor, lighting, noise levels or due to the number of unfamiliar people present. It is essential to interact with people living with dementia in a way that supports them to make sense of their surroundings. Stressors can also be internal – caused by such things as dehydration or constipation.

Repetitive vocalisations in dementia It is important to remember that when a person living with dementia says something, calls out for help or asks a question, this is likely, in their knowledge, to be the first time that they have done so. This is due to the short-term memory loss which occurs in many types of dementia. Providing reassurance and answering questions with the same patience as when they were first asked can support well-being, as can providing the individual with a written note, object or picture through which they can find the reassurance which they are seeking.

Aphasia in dementia A life-changing communication disability which can affect some people with dementia. It is usually progressive and tends to worsen in the middle and later stages of dementia, impairing the person's ability to understand (receptive aphasia) and to use oral and written language (expressive aphasia). It is noteworthy that expressive and receptive aphasia are caused by damage to two distinct areas of the brain. Therefore, a person who has one type of aphasia does not necessarily have the other. In light of this, nursing staff should be mindful that some people who cannot express themselves in words still have complete understanding of what is said to and about them.

Environmental stressors Include noise, light, smells and too much or too little stimulation and can lead to stress and distress for the person living with dementia. Such stress and distress are then likely to be expressed in ways which may not be obviously linked with the root cause, due to the communication challenges that arise as dementia progresses.

Disorientation Describes the inability to correctly acknowledge the current time, place, one's role and personal identity (Schnider, 2012).

Confusion in the ward environment Likely to arise for a person living with dementia because of environmental stressors, inadequate meeting of needs for nutrition, hydration and evacuation of bowels and bladder and misidentification of staff potentially as people who represent a threat. When infection, acute illness and unmanaged pain are added to these, dementia-related disorientation to time and place can easily become compounded by hyper- or hypo-delirium. It is therefore imperative that confusion is not attributed solely to a person's cognitive impairment. Other treatable and manageable causes of confusion should always be considered.

Strengths-based nursing In dementia care this enables family members and the person living with dementia to focus on their individual and group resilience, alongside the enduring skills and attributes of the person diagnosed with dementia, while not looking too far into the future and the deterioration which will inevitably come. This approach *allows for a radical redefinition of the disease by suggesting that positive outcomes are attainable despite difficult circumstances* (McGovern, 2015, p 418).

Need for culturally informed practice Well-established as part of providing safe and effective person-centred care. Culture can be a way of life for some individuals or groups in terms of their behaviours, beliefs, values and attitudes. In its broadest sense it can be linked to a person's heritage or background.

Disabling social environments For people living with dementia, disabling social environments are ones where the person's identity, life history and individual needs are ignored. A key feature of such environments is likely to be the use of malignant social psychology (Kitwood, 1997) as an approach to disempowering and controlling people living with dementia.

Outpacing Where a care provider moves and speaks faster than the person living with dementia can keep up with, including where things are done for and to, rather than with, the person living with dementia. Such outpacing is justified by staff as being quicker than doing things at the pace of the individual. Ultimately, outpacing leads to disempowerment, loss of choice and autonomy, and loss of skills for the person living with dementia.

Cognitive impairment Involves difficulty with processing thoughts. This can include changes in memory, decision-making skills, concentration and attention, and difficulty learning new information.

Recognising the person behind the dementia An essential aspect of providing person-centred dementia care. It includes a recognition of life history and personality, as well as a belief in the endurance of a sense of self-identity in each person living with dementia, however disabled they become as the dementia progresses. See Fazio (2008) for further information on supporting the maintenance of self in the context of dementia.

APPROACHES

Resolving conflict Can be a part of everyday working practice for nurses, depending on the context of service delivery. This can include being a mediator in conflict occurring between patients, as well as seeking to understand people's experience where patients and family members are dissatisfied with the quality of a service. To resolve a conflict, it must be recognised. Avoiding conflict situations potentially only delays facing a difficult situation.

Need for supported nutrition and hydration There are a number of reasons why a person living with dementia may not eat or drink, especially when in an unfamiliar setting. They may not recognise food/drink or be experiencing perceptual changes which make food unappetising. The first step to promoting nutrition and hydration is to ensure the person is aware that food and drink are available and where they are positioned. Make sure that it is something they like, and in a form that they can eat. Creating an environment that triggers eating such as using a tablecloth, napkin and cutlery, and ensuring that others in the environment are also eating, are useful approaches. Avoid watching people eat as this is likely to cause social and psychological discomfort.

Communication In dementia care, communication needs to be individualised and person centred, focused on the abilities of the person living with dementia. Avoid making assumptions about the individual's ability to communicate, as this may fluctuate from day to day, and at different times of the day. Use a strengths-based approach to speak about things which are likely to be familiar to them, and which draw upon long-term autobiographical memory rather than recent events, as a starting point.

Observation skills Can be used with or without validated tools, some of which consist of a straightforward checklist of, for example, actions, behaviours, activities and environmental features to look out for. Checklists for observations tend to be either strengths based or deficit based.

Active listening This is an essential aspect of respecting patients. Becoming an effective listener involves actively engaging with people to make sense of what we see in their body language, in combination with what we hear. We need to hear, consider and process what is said to us in nursing, and this is never a passive process (Ali, 2018).

Standing in their shoes Involves seeing the world from the perspective of the person living with dementia. It may help to sit where they sit for a few minutes, so that you can see and hear what they can, enabling you to literally see the world from their perspective.

Positive communication In the context of dementia care, positive communication is communication which reinforces well-being and a sense of self in the person living with dementia.

Modelling best practice An approach to collaborative and team-based learning in practice settings which is based on learning by observing someone carry out a task and then copying this. It originates from Bandura's (1977) social learning theory which suggests that people are most likely to imitate the behaviours of models they respect and can relate to.

Reflective practice The NMC require reflections as part of the revalidation requirements. Reflection is also an effective starting point for improving nursing practice.

Person-focused versus task-focused care It is essential to recognise the difference between these approaches in all nursing contexts. However, when working with patients living with dementia, person-focused care is central to supporting a strengths-based and empowering approach, which helps people to maintain a sense of self and to continue to be able to participate in their own care.

'This Is Me' A freely downloadable document produced in partnership with the Royal College of Nursing and Alzheimer's Society in the United Kingdom, which is designed to record key information about an individual's past and present needs and preferences. The document should be completed collaboratively with the person living with dementia and with their family members and friends where appropriate.

MODELS

Stages of dementia Often identified as early, middle and late, or sometimes as being recognised across seven stages, up to the point of death. It is noteworthy that no individual is likely to demonstrate all signs of cognitive deterioration according to the delineated progression through stages, as each person living with dementia is unique in terms of how dementia affects them and in how well they can adapt to progressive cognitive impairment.

Non-verbal communication Includes gestures, facial expressions, movements, muscle tension and posture, alongside the volume, tone and pitch of vocalisations. Each person has an individual profile of non-verbal communication, although there may be some culturally and socially derived gestures and expressions which people from similar backgrounds share. Never assume that any aspect of one person's non-verbal communication means the same as a similar or identical gesture on the part of another individual. A key aspect of providing person-centred dementia care is to focus on the individual and what they mean by their non-verbal communication.

Malignant social psychology Outlined by Kitwood (1997) as an approach to interacting with people living with dementia which undermined well-being and personhood, thus leading to all-round deterioration in the individual's experience of life, with the simultaneous progression of neurological impairment.

Positive person work Has been identified as being the opposite of malignant social psychology. The use of positive person work in interactions with people living with dementia leads to the maintenance of personhood, enhanced well-being and an all-round experience of living well with dementia, right up to the point of death, regardless of the progressive neurological damage.

Further reading

Alzheimer's Society (2017) *This Is Me*. [online] Available at: www.alzheimers.org.uk/sites/default/files/migrate/downloads/this_is_me.pdf (accessed 23 February 2023).

Barker, S and Board, M (2012) *Dementia Care in Nursing*. London: Sage.

Baughan, J and Smith, A (2013) *Compassion, Caring and Communication: Skills for Nursing Practice*. 2nd ed. Harlow: Pearson.

Ellis, M and Astell, A (2018) *Adaptive Interaction and Dementia: How to Communicate without Speech*. London: Jessica Kingsley Publishers.

Truswell, D (ed) (2020) *Supporting People Living with Dementia in Black, Asian and Minority Ethnic Communities: Key Issues and Strategies for Change*. London: Jessica Kingsley Publishers.

Yeo, G, Gerdner, L A and Gallagher-Thompson, D (eds) (2019) *Ethnicity and the Dementias*. 3rd ed. Abingdon: Routledge.

Case study 9
Peter: don't miss the point

Sally Hardy

The police come bursting through the double doors. *'Careful with this one love, you might want to remove all flammable objects from the area!'* joked the first uniformed officer. They were referring to the fact alcohol could be smelt emanating from the person on the ambulance trolley before I could even see them. The trolley was being pushed by two ambulance crew in their bright-yellow fluorescent jackets. The blue flashing lights of the ambulance, mixed with the police car headlights in the background, were a distraction at first until my line of sight caught a blood-splattered head, matted with hair just visible beneath the thin blanket. It was 3am on a Wednesday morning in January in the emergency department (ED). This was no weekend partygoer having had one too many, I thought to myself.

APPROACH: inter-agency working

APPROACH: assessment

'Through here please', I shouted to the crew so they could locate the empty bay prepped and awaiting the new admission. It had been called through 15 minutes earlier as an unknown male, 40–50 years of age, head injury, found on the heath, cold and unresponsive. I took a more detailed handover from the ambulance crew who had tended to the wounds where they had found him on site and undertaken an initial assessment.

APPROACH: pre-hospital care

'Okay, so... we think this is a Peter Wilburton. That's the name in a wallet in his jacket pocket. A Caucasian male, aged between 40 and 50, found on the heath near Wyebridge Waters, unconscious and cold. Estimate he was outside for several hours; body was found by a night fishing group who phoned for the ambulance and police. They thought he was dead or had been mugged. We got to the scene at 3.07am, found a faint pulse and blood from laceration to the head. Strong smell of alcohol and several tins of special brew in a plastic bag were beside the body. No other form of identification except a local library card in the wallet where we got the name. Pulse steady but faint, blood loss from the head, no other body lacerations identified. Wound site is a 14cm wide laceration across brow area, over both eyes, sustained from what must have been a head on fall against the adjacent concrete wall. Intravenous saline infusion started on site – has had 500ml of a

APPROACH: history taking

MODEL: drug and alcohol intoxication

1 litre bag. Dialled through to you at 3.34 and delivery at 03.04am Wednesday 14th January, not bad work hey'.

By the time the verbal handover was complete, we had moved Peter onto an ED trolley; the doctor beside me was already checking pupil dilation and starting a head-to-toe assessment while the crew member talked. I had strapped Peter's left arm to the haemodynamic monitoring system and started the machine which beeped away gathering our first set of observations. A soft neck brace the ambulance crew had used was left in place until we knew more of the extent of the head injury.

APPROACH: cervical spine immobilisation

APPROACHES: assessment – coma scale/amnesia; inter-agency working

'Thanks. Anything else? Any sign of seizures or fitting? Why not a mugging? Will the police stick around?' I asked.

THEORY: diagnostic overshadowing

'No, doubt it – there was no sign of a struggle, no other footprints in the mud, pattern of blood spillage matched where he'd hit the wall. My guess is he is a local out on the razzle who had one too many tonight', replied the crew member.

I looked up at the crew member – *'Oh, okay. Thanks for the tip off'*. We smiled at each other, as a shorthand for saying goodbye as they both left the curtained off-bay, leaving the doctor and me to do our work. Apart from the bleep from the monitor, it was suddenly quiet. I noticed his breathing was getting shallow, and the pulse rate was continuing to drop. I looked over at the doctor. *'Do you think there is risk of other internal damage, internal bleeding?'* I said. *'Get some bloods tests and get me an ECG'*, the doctor responded. I was already outside of the curtains bringing in the ECG machine and calling to my colleagues at the desk to take blood tests. While applying the ECG leads across the legs, chest and arms, I cursed internally... *why doesn't anyone ever put these leads back properly!* I sighed while untangling the web of wires so I could attach them in the correct order.

APPROACH: assessment

MODEL: technical know-how

Those initial few minutes when receiving a patient can be crucial, and it is important not to miss the key points of a holistic assessment. I was used to working with the on-call doctor that night. We had an unspoken agreement where direct eye contact meant things were getting serious. We had barely glanced at each other, going through our routine checks separately yet together like a dance. I knew with Peter that we were not yet out of the woods; he was a physically strong-looking chap, so we could pull him back, I was certain. The ECG showed no abnormalities, as if confirming my intuitive assessment.

APPROACH: inter-professional working

THEORY: forms of knowing

I started cleaning the facial wounds and could see bruising appear in front of me as the caked-on dried blood was removed and the puffy swollen skin across his forehead remained red and pliable. Both eyes were swollen shut, but no blood was coming from the tear ducts so hopefully I was wrong and there was no intercranial bleeding.

The doctor's clinical assessment and Glasgow Coma Score indicated no further investigations were required tonight, so we sutured the large laceration across his forehead, and I finished off by bandaging his head, making him look more like a wartime soldier than a drunk found on the heath.

Peter started to rouse at about 6am, struggling to open his eyes due to the harsh lighting in the ED trolley bay. I told him he was in hospital, and I was the nurse looking after him. *'What's your name?'* he said. *'Sally'*, I replied. *'Marry me Sally'*, he slurred. *'Well, that was quick'*, I replied. *'You haven't set eyes on me yet!'*

By 7am he was fully awake and sat up with a cup of tea and some toast the healthcare assistant had organised for him. I came back to check on him and started to see the person behind the injuries. *'Morning'*, I chirped as I came round the curtains, noticing his facial skin colour was less pale. *'Sally is my darlin, my darlin, my darlin'*, he sang to me, as I noted down the observations and checked his bandage for any leaking. *'You bounce back nicely'*, I replied. *'What happened to you last night?'*

'Can't remember' was his quick retort.

'Shall I remind you?' I asked.

'Nope' came the response.

I bustled about some more. *'I only came in to stop smoking'*, he said. *'Well, you could have got a patch from the chemists instead of bashing your head open'*, I suggested rather sarcastically. He scoffed.

'More tea, nurse!' he demanded, changing the subject.

'I'd like a please?' I said, writing my notes on the patient record sheets at the end of his trolley but keeping an eye on his mood changes, wondering if this was a result of the head injury or something else.

'Pretty pleeeease.' He smiled broadly at me. His teeth were stained from tobacco and caffeine; one of the front ones was cracked, but otherwise not a bad set.

I went to get a fresh cup of tea, giving me time to think through what else I needed to know before I handed over to the day shift.

'Here you go, Peter', I said, as I handed him the plastic beaker of tea. *'Any sugar?'*

'How do you know me?' he asked.

'Your wallet, I put it in that bag with your jacket and clothes', I said, pointing to a white plastic hospital property bag on the chair in the corner.

'No really, how do you know me?' His voice was serious this time.

'What do you mean – as a person – as a patient?' I asked.

'If I told you stuff, you'd lock me away', he said flatly.

'So, there's things you want to tell me?' I replied. *'How long you got?'* he snapped back.

At that point I had to make a decision. Do I probe further, or do I let the day shift unravel this complicated person propped up in the bed in front of me beginning to reveal more of his character. I sat down on the side of the bed.

'I don't have long but I am here now. What did you want to say?'

'I want to give up smoking, I can't do it anymore. No one is helping me; I need to take the voices away. Smoking makes them worse. It feeds them. Help me please, or else they will slowly and pain-fully kill me.'

'Okay Peter – it is Peter, isn't it?' He nods. I say, *'I can't stay long now, but I will get someone to come and speak with you who can help you. I think you have come to the right place but first let us freshen you up to receive all the visitors coming to find you. Is there anyone you want me to contact to tell them you are here?'* *'No one'*, he replied.

Reflections

There is no normal shift when working in ED. For many that is part of the attraction of not really knowing what will come through the door. This patient was no different to many others I had dealt with, yet the handover given by the ambulance crew and the police presence made me think there was more to this person than the initial presentation.

The immediacy of saving lives in ED meant that it is a priority in this scenario to assess and manage the head injury. Peter had been outside in January, so we had to warm the body, allowing all the internal organs to fully function, and to ensure any risk of permanent damage was alleviated promptly.

As a dual-qualified adult and mental health nurse, it was clear I was the right person to be present as Peter began to explain his actions. I was not put off by his mention of voices in his head. I should have noticed the early clues in the initial handover, in terms of the bash to the front of the head on a concrete wall – was this deliberate self-harm? Being isolated and near water – was this a planned suicide attempt that had gone wrong?

My reflections 'in action' were based on my years of clinical experience, which allowed me to use every opportunity to assess and adapt my interventions with Peter. Admittedly, I had at first seen him as a drunk who had fallen over. But taking in all the information and watching him as the effects of the alcohol wore off, his initial interactions led me to think there was a personality and character here who was seeking a human connection. He admitted to having no family or next of kin for me to contact, and was charming me with his cheeky marriage proposal, big grin and a childlike plea for more tea.

The importance of a brief encounter in ED can provide a confessional atmosphere. The person has found somewhere safe, someone to help them, paying them individual and full attention. Even physical touch, through basic care such as wound dressing and regular observations, can all create an environment of intimacy. I used this physical space to give Peter my time and attention, building a rapport and providing a safe space for him to feel comfortable enough to share more of his story.

I was not expecting to hear about his internal voices. At this early stage of assessment, I was unclear whether this was alcohol induced, or a depressive or schizoid psychosis. I needed someone else to speak with him in more detail and to undertake a full mental state examination, which I did not have the time to achieve at the end of a busy night shift. I also suspected, after hearing him express his fear of being locked up, that the head injury might not have been an accident. There was far more to Peter's story than I got to hear that night.

Questions for reflection and discussion

1. What do different professional perspectives bring when aiming to understand the process of assessment and managing patients across and in different situations, settings and contexts?

2. What can busy professionals do to more effectively fully understand their patients amid the numerous interruptions and distractions in health and social care settings?

3. How can practitioners keep themselves aware of potential early warning signs when working with people at their most vulnerable?

4. What approaches can a person use to better understand someone who is expressing suicidal thoughts?

5. When is it best to refer a patient on to other professional personnel?

6. Why is it important to be reflective and self-aware as a professional practitioner?

Further information

VALUES

Prejudice/unconscious bias Each person has been brought up to understand the world they live in from those around them, who have influenced their thinking. These influences can become strongly associated with our behaviours, choices, interactions and decision making, where we seek out people, places and things that are familiar to us. Stereotyping, prejudice and associated traits can form unconscious responses when seeing something unfamiliar. This can become identified as an unconscious bias but informs how we respond and react to people unfamiliar to us. Stigma and bias, whether conscious or at an unconscious subliminal level, can cause considered harm, disparity and disharmony when working and engaging in a multicultural society. There is a considerable risk of unconscious bias associated with professional groups who make rapid decisions based on information and evidence placed in front of them. Using self-reflection and having a commitment to identifying and determining your own biases can help to surface any discrimination, microaggressions and negative attitudes.

Getting to know the person Focusing attention on the person as a whole, not just their physical or mental state, is an important value-based approach to delivering care that is right for that person. Understanding the person is central to getting the care right for them and adapting approaches to suit their situation and preferences. Getting to know the person, and their likes and dislikes, allows for close relationships to form quite quickly between a patient and their carer, allowing that person to be heard, valued and accepted for who they are, unique in their own lives.

Communication Effective communication and working with others is an essential element of any healthcare setting and teamwork. Communication can affect patient safety, and when communication breaks down, this is often at the core of clinical incidents. Understanding the exchange of information between people, where and how this can be strengthened, and where and how it can break down are core components of effective and safe clinical practice. Communication includes having a keen awareness of how you interact with others and can be enhanced when you are effectively listening and using questioning (John Heron's (2001) six-category interventions are a very useful framework) to undertake your assessment and form an ongoing working relationship with a person.

Use of humour It is important to understand the person before using humour as it can be offensive to some, while it also can be a useful tool, when used well, that promotes connection, compassion, understanding and helps to reduce stressful situations. Humour can shift the sympathetic nervous system to a parasympathetic response, which can reduce fear and pain thresholds by releasing endorphins.

Open questioning There are multiple forms of questioning, and the most effective way of obtaining information from someone is to ask open questions rather than closed questions that only require a yes or no response.

Confirmation/empathy Most often associated with being non-judgemental, confirmation of a person is about acceptance and showing empathy for their situation and circumstance by acknowledging something and remaining neutral or unbiased in what you are hearing, feeling or speaking about. Confirmation does not mean tolerance; it is instead a conscious decision to become aware of a situation and spend time understanding and exploring it further. Once that fuller awareness and understanding has been reached, then informed decisions as to what needs to happen next can be agreed.

THEORIES

Diagnostic overshadowing This can occur when symptoms of physical illness or the presenting symptoms are focused upon rather than seeking an underlying or associated complication. This can cause severe delay in obtaining the correct treatments, and can leave patients dissatisfied with their care and professionals frustrated that their patients are being difficult or problematic. Preventing this from happening requires staff to undertake holistic assessments and reflect continually on their attitudes, skills, education and practice. Sheila Hardy's book (Hardy, 2022) is a great text for ensuring both physical and mental health issues have parity of esteem.

Forms of knowing Carper's (1978) four ways of knowing outlines how practitioners use different sources of knowledge and has been applied well to nursing expertise. It is a typology that has four patterns of knowing that a person uses: 1) empirical or factual knowledge; 2) personal knowledge and experiences gained; 3) ethical or moral awareness often built over time through cultural and social influences; 4) aesthetic or intuitive knowledge, is the ability to attribute prior knowledge to a situation, and is a unique blend of all forms of understanding.

Physiology A science that aims to understand how the body functions and interacts with its internal and external environment. It helps to understand what the normal functions of the human body are, from which you can then identify where and how things start to go wrong.

Person centredness As a theory was developed by Carl Rogers (1979) to help understand life from an individual's perspective, as a unique and expressive experience influenced by conditions and our personal relationships with the world and others within it.

APPROACHES

Inter-agency working When more than one agency or professional discipline work together in a planned and formal way to ensure the patient pathway remains joined up and cohesive, maximising potential for positive outcomes, effective communication is key. Being clear in terms of what you need to know, and how you can in return share pertinent and relevant information clearly, is important to consider so that ongoing inter-agency working will achieve the best outcomes for the patient. Despite this good intention, some professional groups do not share the same language or values, which can lead to fractured or difficult working across professional and service boundaries. In the current political re-configuration of integrated care systems, it is important for inter-agency working to achieve improvements for population health and social cohesion. However, much research is still needed to emphasise what and how best practice can be achieved within a limited public financial envelope.

Assessment Assessment is a process that is a basic requirement of healthcare practitioners, particularly when undertaking an effective valid assessment of the patient's health status, which is important to then inform and formulate appropriate interventions from which to prevent further clinical changes. Using standardised assessment tools and approaches can help with providing standardised terminology to use with other professional groups when providing care for a patient with complex care needs.

Pre-hospital care Many people sustain head injuries per year, many of which do not require medical treatment. Health promotion strategies for enabling people to avoid common risks that lead to sustained head injury and subsequent medical interventions can have long-lasting effects on the person's life. Paramedics will have undertaken training in Advanced Life Support (ATLS) courses and how to pass on essential information to the emergency department personnel, providing key information on signs and symptoms and outlining their initial course of action to stabilise the person prior to moving them to hospital.

History taking An important aspect of assessment is taking a history of the person from a medical perspective to understand what medication and surgery they have had, plus a family history mapping both existing and potential patterns of disease and a social history such as smoking, drinking, drug taking and any other issue that might inform a picture of the person's health risks.

Cervical spine immobilisation This is an initial safety measure used for immediate treatment of any suspected spinal injury and is identified as the safest way of preventing any secondary injury during transportation of the patient. A cervical collar is placed around the patient's neck, and care is taken to avoid further risk of damage by keeping the patient's spine in alignment with minimal handling.

Assessment – coma scales/amnesia The risk following a head injury of increased intracranial pressure brings added complications and can cause a loss of consciousness and/or amnesia. Monitoring the neurological signs and symptoms over time, using evidence-based scales (such as the Glasgow Coma Scale) can help assess the level of internal problems that need external interventions (such as surgery). Using scales from which to assess a head injury/cervical spine immobilisation provides the assessment process an informed and valid tool from which to indicate the patient's physical status. The use of early warning signs and having an understanding of physiological changes are both important and core clinical competences. All patients with suspected or actual head trauma, or a Glasgow Coma Score of less than or equal to 8, will have their neck supported to immobilise the cervical spine, avoiding further injury and potential paralysis. If clinical assessment is to include imaging using a CT scan or X-ray, the immobilisation device needs to remain until it is deemed safe to remove it. The Glasgow Coma Scale is a standardised system for assessing the degree of brain impairment. There are three determinants: 1) eye opening, 2) verbal response and 3) motor responses. Each is evaluated independently, and a numerical value is given to indicate the level of consciousness and degree of dysfunction.

Inter-professional working Similar to inter-agency working (as outlined above), inter-professional working allows practitioners to work together to co-ordinate care for patients, based on their professional training and scope of practice. Working in collaboration is an important aspect of effective teamwork and is achieved when each discipline understands what their expertise can bring to a situation and is seen to improve quality outcomes for the patient.

Assessment – wound care Assessing the state of a patient's wound is a fundamental element of minimising infection and maximising the healing process. There are two different classifications of a wound, one being an acute wound, which is most often because of a surgical wound or traumatic injury. This sort of wound is expected to heal within four weeks due to the natural inflammatory response occurring to close the wound. A more chronic wound is one where the healing process is delayed or incomplete, which may be due to more systemic problems such as medications or even inappropriate dressing and treatment.

Assessment of mental/physical safety For some people, standardised risk assessments are reductive and restrictive, whereas professional intuition has been valued as using all forms of knowledge in your clinical risk assessment. This incorporates both physical scanning (as outlined above) and the ability to also assess a person's mental state from their interactions and responses to your interventions with them, whether through questioning or observing the person and picking up clues. It is important to have a checklist in mind so that you do not miss things, which is the focus of this case study. For example, if the person is saying they want to harm themselves, make sure you remove from their reach any equipment or objects that will allow them to do this. Any concerns should be reported and followed up with the team to ensure you have shared the risk with others and minimised any harm that can come to the patient. However, do not feel you have to be able to do everything as it is important to remain within your scope of practice. The holistic assessment process is something nurses are trained to achieve through a continuous and repeated process of informed practice and decision making, based on the knowledge, skills and attributes of the practitioner, incorporating foundational understanding of biomedical and psychosocial sciences. It is further informed by nurses' professional values and applied in their professional scope of practice. For many nurse theorists, holistic practice includes consideration of spiritual dimensions alongside mind and body connections.

Accurate documentation/record keeping This is not only a professional standard and code of conduct requirement but also a legal aspect of the work we do as practitioners. Maintaining good and accurate records not only helps other professionals to get up to date quickly with a person's status and your assessment of that person, but it also allows for the organisation to have a record of procedures that have been undertaken.

Self-care indicators Another key aspect of assessment is observing the person's state of health through their presentation, whether it is the clothes they are wearing, the cleanliness of their hair and nails, or the state of their dental health. All of these can be used to identify whether the individual is looking after themselves or being cared for by others. Basic hygiene is a good indicator of a person's well-being and state of health.

Non-threatening body language A useful technique for overcoming barriers in a professional setting is to physically place yourself at an equal height to the other person's eye level. For example, you can reduce the emphasis of power by standing over a person who is in a more vulnerable setting, such as sitting or lying down. This is a simple attempt to level the relationship between the patient and the professional. It can also be used to defuse potential fear and anxiety through indicating to the person that you are on their side and willing to meet them as an equal. This approach should be used in conjunction with assessing the situation, ensuring there is no physical risk of harm to either person.

Scope of practice The Nursing and Midwifery Council (NMC) is the body that ensures practitioners have a professional standard of knowledge, skills and aptitudes that are mapped out within their sphere or scope of practice. As a healthcare professional, undertaking activities beyond your scope of practice is unsafe, and therefore means you are working outside of a legal framework of protection that not only puts yourself at risk, but it is also increasing a risk of harm to others. Therefore, if you are unsure of your scope of practice, refer the situation on to someone else to help you make an informed decision as to the next course of action to take, for the best interests of your patient.

Distraction/questioning This is a useful approach to questioning, particularly if the person is beginning to focus on something that is increasing their anxiety or making them agitated and potentially at risk of being violent or aggressive. This is a common approach used with children to take their mind off having an injection or can be used as a strategy when undertaking a wound-cleaning procedure or removing a cannula, so that the person is distracted from the activity they are fearful of. The technique of distraction can also help to build a picture of the person, finding out more about their interests or, as in this case study, identifying whether they have any next of kin that need to be contacted.

MODELS

Drug and alcohol intoxication The amount of alcohol consumed and certain types of medications can interfere with a person's level of consciousness, and side effects can include vomiting, headaches and amnesia, plus speech and movement impairment (loss of balance). Vomiting and fitting can also be associated with drug and alcohol intoxication, and therefore assessment of these symptoms on their own is not the best form of assessment associated with a head injury. Irritability or altered behaviour can also be confused with a post-head-injury assessment process.

Technical know-how An approach to undertaking a task based on methods or techniques that are practically performed. Many technical skills require training and a level of competency is measured to indicate the ability to perform the task safely and efficiently. It is often a model of care delivery that is seen in healthcare as competency based.

Person-centred practice Advances in practice and emergence of new person-centred thinking, practices, methods and tools brings a contemporary focus of being and remaining person centred to maximise health and well-being outcomes. McCormack and McCance (2016) have written extensively about person-centred practices for healthcare settings.

Brief encounters/every contact counts Often in healthcare settings, a person is only in your care for a brief period; this can be identified as a brief encounter but still provides opportunity to understand their situation and assess their level of need. Using that time to make sure you have influenced their health and well-being is an approach to public service working that involves engaging in the provision of health promotion, advice and prevention as part of everyday interactions. Shepard (2012) offers an overview of the model from an evidence-based review.

Reflective practice Enables practitioners to remain conscious of their own beliefs, values and practices, demanding conscious effort and guided facilitation to enable improved patient care. Ongoing research shows that practitioners need to not only reflect on their practice, but should also be reflecting in action, and for action improvements at every opportunity. Patel and Metersky's (2022) paper provides a good reference for understanding more about the importance of reflective practice.

Counselling/echoing A talking therapy approach to providing a person with professional help and guidance for resolving their personal problems. There are many different models of counselling, drawing on different theoretical underpinnings. One of the core components of all counselling relationships is establishing the boundaries of that relationship and building rapport between the two parties to ensure that the working relationship will remain therapeutic, helpful and separate from other relationships the person is seeking. One approach to show you are listening intently is to echo the same words being used by the person when seeking additional information about their understanding of an issue they have raised with you.

Suicidal ideation A public health issue where a person becomes preoccupied with plans or repeated attempts to take their own life. A staggering number of people each year experience these suicidal thoughts. Better identification and more effective treatments to prevent suicide is an ongoing issue of concern and external factors, as well as mental and physical health, can influence a person's determination to end their life. There are numerous clinical guidelines and each person's situation needs to be considered when working with them to challenge this approach to their situation or crisis. There are many people who can help if you have been affected by this case study or are yourself having suicidal thoughts. See Mind (2020).

Further reading

Alkhaqani, A L (2022) Importance of Teamwork Communication in Nursing Practice. *Nurse Communication*, 6: 1–2.

Byermoen, K R, Eide, T, Egilsdottir, H Ö, Eide, H, Heyn, L G, Moen, A and Brembo, E A (2022) Nursing Students' Development of Using Physical Assessment in Clinical Rotation—a Stimulated Recall Study. *BioMedical Central: Nursing*, 21(1): 1–17.

Marcelin, J R, Siraj, D S, Victor, R, Kotadia, S and Maldonado, Y A (2019) The Impact of Unconscious Bias in Healthcare: How to Recognize and Mitigate It. *The Journal of Infectious Diseases*, 220 (Supplement 2): S62–S73.

Mind (2020) Suicidal Feelings. [online] Available at: www.mind.org.uk/information-support/types-of-mental-health-problems/suicidal-feelings/about-suicidal-feelings (accessed 23 February 2023).

Molloy, R, Brand, G, Munro, I and Pope, N (2021) Seeing the Complete Picture: A Systematic Review of Mental Health Consumer and Health Professional Experiences of Diagnostic Overshadowing. *Journal of Clinical Nursing*.

Potter, P J and Frisch, N (2007) Holistic Assessment and Care: Presence in the Process. *Nursing Clinics of North America*, 42(2): 213–28.

Case study 10
Scarlet: cutting, coping and compassion

Louise Cherrill and Sarah Housden

The phone starts ringing. I stare at it for a while as if I can will away the referral by not answering straightaway. *'Another one for us? Okay – I'm on my way.'* As I head downstairs, I reflect on how busy the shift has been, and how many referrals we have had. I wonder what creative private space the emergency department (ED) staff will find for me to complete my assessment this time, knowing that they are full to bursting.

'What have we got?' I say to the charge nurse.

'Self-inflicted cuts, cubicle 4. Can you take it in the family room? I need that space for an emergency that will be here in five minutes.'

'What's their name?' I ask the charge nurse. She stares at me, irritated, shuffles the papers in front of her and says, *'Scarlet, their name is Scarlet. She does not want to talk to us or tell us what happened. I can see from the notes it looks like she had some news about her care team changing today; she's probably here to manipulate the situation'*.

VALUE: patient-centred care

THEORY: transitions in care

VALUE: communication

Outwardly, I smile, and say *'Okay – I'll see what I can do'*, but inwardly frustration is pulsing through me at the lack of resources, training and understanding leading to these judgements that influence the experiences of care for those who harm themselves. My dilemma is that a positive approach to working with someone who has harmed themselves is perceived negatively by my colleagues who consider the patient a *'time waster'* and that while I am listening to her, I am potentially neglecting the needs of other patients that are in an ED which is working under extreme pressure. Therefore, my approach to understanding the patient's experience is unsustainable. I know this is not Scarlet's first time in the ED and, due to having been treated in an off-hand way on previous occasions, I am not surprised the ED staff think she is particularly withdrawn and uncommunicative.

APPROACH: trauma-informed care

THEORY: active listening

VALUES: communication; efficient and effective care

THEORY: revolving door syndrome

MODEL: prevention

VALUE: judgements and assumptions

I scan through the notes so I am not walking in blind. Scarlet is 24 and has been under the children and younger people's mental

APPROACH: history taking

| MODEL: care-coordination |

| THEORY: therapeutic relationships |

| MODEL: The Medical Model |

| VALUE: empathy and compassion |

| MODEL: DBT |

| THEORIES: organisational cultures; self-harm |

| VALUE: 'Hello, my name is' campaign |

| VALUE: non-judgemental |

| APPROACH: multidisciplinary team working |

| THEORY: cognitive dissonance |

| THEORY: burnout |

health services for most of her life. She has had the same care-coordinator for ten of those years and the notes suggest she just found out that she is being transferred to the Adult Community Mental Health Team.

Scarlet also has a diagnosis of emotionally unstable personality disorder (EUPD). There are strong reactions to this label.

- Fear– fear of the risk of harm to self, fear of being manipulated and fear of the intensity of the emotions that will be laid before you.

- Contempt – contempt for the person's place within services; contempt for the amount of time that is perceived to be spent with these service users; and even more contempt as the behaviours repeat despite the huge efforts by their teams and the idea that they are stuck in a revolving door.

Yet, since undertaking my training in dialectical behavioural therapy (DBT) I feel a deep sadness at the lack of understanding of the causes of EUPD and the ways to manage it. Perhaps the most frightening aspect of EUPD is the repeated serious self-harm and suicide attempts that bring people like Scarlet to the ED.

I stand by the cubicle curtain and take a deep breath, but the words catch in my throat and I have to breathe again.

'Hello Scarlet? My name is Sophie. Can I come in?'

Scarlet looks up at me and then quickly looks back to her lap.

'Why?'

'I am from the mental health liaison service; I have come to talk to you about why you're here today and how I might be able to help'.

'I'm here to waste your time and take up a bed – that's what you think, isn't it?' is her reply.

I am slightly taken back by her honesty and the conviction with which she demonstrates how worthless and undeserving of our time she feels. I feel inner discomfort as I wonder how many negative experiences have left her feeling like this. Simultaneously, I understand the frustrations behind my colleagues' behaviour which will have underpinned the previous interactions. I know that I too, before now, have felt that level of frustration that can be so difficult to mask from your service users.

'I think you're here because...' I pick up her chart. *'I think you're here because you need some stitches in your arm. Can you tell me what happened?'*

Recognising that self-harm can be a coping mechanism for people who have experienced difficult or traumatic experiences in early life, I work with her to try to understand what has brought her to a place where self-harm feels like the only way to cope with the intense feelings arising from a lifetime of trauma.

Scarlet explains that she found out today that her care is being transferred to the Adult Community Mental Health Team. She feels an overwhelming sadness and sense of loss at this change. Having been taken into care when she was younger, with multiple foster home and school changes, the only consistent relationship she has is that which she has formed with her care-coordinator, and therefore understandably there is a strong attachment. I validate her sadness. Scarlet seems surprised. She says *'It's okay to feel sad!? I HATE feeling sad. I am angry you think it is okay I feel sad!'*

There is a misconception about emotions. That we have good emotions and bad emotions. That we should only feel those that are good, or that we should not feel sad or angry. This idea is drummed into us from an early age – the perceived unacceptability of subsequent external control of emotional expression during the *'terrible twos'* or during *'teenage angst'* which we gradually learn to regulate through self-imposed censorship of socially unacceptable behaviours and feelings. Such internal censorship is subsequently reinforced by social media posts projecting images of perfection, which make us believe that if we are not perfect, or if we do not feel perfect, then we are less than human.

I explain that emotions are inbuilt methods of communication; they tell us helpful things and provide useful urges for us to act on. Scarlet is wilful, a term we use in dialectical behaviour therapy when a service user is resistant to change. She shoots back, *'How could sadness possibly be useful? The only urge it gave me was to cut!'* I tell her what I think. *'Sadness tells us you have lost something, and you are losing the good relationship with your care-co that you have built up over a long time. It has*

VALUE: professionalism

THEORY: adverse childhood experiences (ACEs)

VALUE: unconditional positive regard

THEORIES: coping mechanisms; emotional overwhelm

APPROACH: working with looked after children

THEORY: attachment, separation

VALUE: acceptance

APPROACH: validation

THEORIES: emotional regulation; socialisation

MODEL: social and emotional development

THEORY: compliance with social norms

APPROACH: health education

made you withdraw to protect yourself from further losses, it has made you cry to communicate to others that you are sad, and, it has brought you here so we can offer you extra support.' 'You are angry because I have threatened the perception you have of yourself by validating what you feel are "negative" emotions.'

Scarlet articulates herself well, but she tells me 'I am used to being made to feel stupid for not being able to control my emotions'. Her intense displays of anger and sadness are negatively reinforced by the removal of care, which feeds into her belief she is not worthy. She struggles with this unpredictable emotional dysregulation. She is particularly sensitive to her emotions, and yet she grew up in a family that expected her to hide all her feelings. I explain the biosocial model to her, as an explanation of her difficulties, and I can visibly see the relief in her face as she understands there is a cause she finds acceptable for what she is feeling. All the behaviours we see (thoughts, feelings, emotions) are Scarlet's attempts to regulate her emotions in the best way she can, given her life experiences.

I need to come to a decision about her risk and whether she can go home. Scarlet says she has suicidal thoughts – she does not want to wake up in the morning – but that these are always there. She has no current plans to end her life, and her intent with her self-harm is to manage her emotions. This is common, but it causes professional anxiety because of the fear of accidental death, so I know I'll want to talk through the decision I make now with my line manager and colleagues. I ask her, 'When you go home, do you think you can keep yourself safe?' This question makes me feel sick in the pit of my stomach as I put the responsibility for safety back onto Scarlet. Even if she says 'no', the options are limited. Scarlet states that she can keep herself safe, but I want to spend a bit more time doing some safety planning with her. I can feel the eyes of the nurses wanting the space piercing into the back of my head like daggers.

I want to understand what sort of things trigger Scarlet's thoughts of self-harm, what support she has available to her, and what, if any, alternatives she tries before she acts on the urges to cut. Scarlet explains to me that any intense emotion leaves her feeling like a bottle of coke that has been dropped down the stairs – like she is going to explode – but with no way of taking the lid off. For her, cutting allows her to remove the lid in a way that reduces all the pressure and resets her pressure gauge. I reflect on how often I, and my colleagues, have felt like this at the end of a shift that feels like a nightmare. I also think of how our ways of taking the lids off – eating an entire pizza, a nice bottle of something, a long run, a marathon computer gaming session on our day off, or 20 cigarettes a day – are also damaging to our body but do not come with the same social unacceptability and therefore judgement. Over time, we may put ourselves into a different area of the health service with these behaviours and so will – hopefully – not be the recipients of this kind of negative attention, being scrutinised by our ED colleagues in the same way that Scarlet is.

Scarlet does not feel that she can talk to her friends about her feelings. She tells me she does not have a safe space to talk about what goes on in her head because talking about wanting to cut herself, even if she does not intend to act on these thoughts, tends to worry her friends and cause overreaction. We talk about the different support agencies she could contact instead and I give her the phone numbers, but this almost feels like ticking a box to be able to write the risk assessment later. I am not confident that she will actually use them, however much she needs them.

APPROACH: recognising the need for support for unpaid carers

THEORY: social stigma

I want Scarlet to leave our assessment with something practical she can use when she is having these feelings. *'If you tell me to have a bath or a nice cup of tea, I'm liable to lump you one'*, she says. I laugh. We tend to come back to these same superficial ideas for solutions repeatedly – which do nothing to combat the urge to self-harm but reflect the lack of intervention training, and therefore the lack of confidence, experienced by too many of our team members. I assure her that I am not going to give her this kind of advice; as much as a nice hot bath is good for our wellbeing, it might not help in the moment of emotional crisis. I talk to her about the STOP skill. Stop – Take a step back and breathe; Observe – Proceed mindfully. Scarlet rolls her eyes at me. *'How is that going to help me?'* she says. *'It will give you the time and space you need to make sure that you are not acting blindly on your emotions. It will give you a moment to soothe yourself, to think about what has happened to make you feel how you feel, and to problem solve it. Time to move forward in a way that is safe.'* If the urge is still there, as she is not on any heart or blood pressure medication, I advise her to plunge her face into a bowl of cold water, the 'TIPP skill'. We talk about the physiological processes triggered, stopping what is going on in her body and helping the way she feels, so that the urge to self-harm subsides.

VALUE: patient empowerment

APPROACH: distraction

VALUE: competence

APPROACH: dialectical behaviour therapy

THEORY: self-soothing

APPROACH: patient safety

THEORY: parasympathetic nervous system

We chat for a while longer, and then Scarlet is declared medically fit to go home. A friend is coming to collect her. She thanks me for my time, and for giving her space to just talk. I head back to my office to try and capture this interaction in the notes.

As I finish my notes, glance at my watch and realise it has been several hours since I got myself a drink, I head to the kitchen. I have a heavy feeling behind my eyes as if I am getting a head-ache – today has been draining. I walk in and am shocked to see the charge nurse leaning on the counter, crying. She is equally shocked at having been disturbed. We briefly stare at each other unsure what to do next.

'*Are you okay?*' I hold my breath, waiting to see where this goes.

'*I am just so burnt out!*' she exclaims. '*I am overwhelmed at the volume of patients we are expected to see, and I am angry that when we are so busy, we have people here who have intentionally hurt themselves.*'

I take a deep breath. '*I understand.*'

'*You do?*' she says, surprised.

'*Yes, your anger is valid*', I try to reassure her.

She does not understand how I can spend so much one-to-one time with service users who have self-harmed while also understanding her anger. I smile to myself, as I grappled with this concept for such a long time myself.

I explain – '*your anger is valid because it is telling you that you are blocked in pursuit of your goals of an emergency department that meets its targets and key performance indicators. Your ability to be the best charge nurse you can be is threatened. Anger communicates this to us. It gives us the motivation and energy we need to work through these challenges. If you felt nothing, you would not have the urge to problem solve as you do now; that is stemming from your anger*'.

She looks at me, stating she had never understood anger as useful before. '*But what about the service users?*'

I smile again, as I say '*dialectics*' and she looks at me like I am crazy.

'Two things, two opposites, opposing things, black and white, existing at the same time. It feels uncomfortable, the cognitive dissonance is real, but you can simultaneously be angry about your goals for running your department being blocked, while also providing compassionate person-centred care, making the service user feel heard and valued, understanding that both your and their emotions are valid. We all have judgement thoughts; the key is being mindful and recognising what is a judgement thought and what is a fact. There are lots of judgement thoughts about self-harm: that it is manipulative, that it is attention-seeking, that it is an attempt at suicide. Self-harm is a highly secretive behaviour that is generally used to manage overwhelming emotion that would otherwise lead to a suicide attempt. Those who are self-harming are trying really hard to stay alive! When we think about control, it can be used as a way to feel in control when nothing else does, rather than as a technique to control someone else.'

APPROACH: harm minimisation

We reflect for a while. The space for reflective practice has decreased as the demands on our time increase but its importance has not diminished.

APPROACH: reflective practice

I head back up to the office to do my notes and GP letter. This is my final chance to demonstrate compassion, understanding and validation to Scarlet, thinking carefully about the words that I use and mindfully describing the behavioural facts of our interaction without attaching judgement or inferences to what occurred.

VALUE: record keeping

VALUE: unconditional positive regard

I look at the time again; my shift ended an hour ago. My heart is heavy with others' problems and yet I feel lighter for having lightened their loads. I mindfully drive home, concentrating on my driving, to leave the stress from the day at work so I can complete that all-important self-care when I arrive home.

APPROACH: self-care

Reflections

Looking back on my work with Scarlet, I feel satisfied that I did the best I could for her within the small window of space and time that exists in the emergency department. While I know that my interactions and intervention with Scarlet seem minimal compared to the trauma of her past experiences and ongoing distress, I can also see that it is in moments like these that nurses can potentially make a significant difference to the futures of patients who otherwise receive little or no constructive guidance on how to manage emotions which feel like they are out of control. To know that their feelings can be understood and acknowledged as valid by another person can make such a difference to people who may have come to see themselves as beyond help. If we could get such service provision developed to its full potential, we would most likely reduce the current demand for more extensive mental health interventions within emergency departments.

My work with Scarlet, and others like her, leaves me wanting to see some radical changes in the way healthcare services are delivered, and I think that requires a radical reconceptualisation about who is, or is not, in need of healthcare – including a move away from ideas about there being worthy or unworthy patients. Consideration also needs to be given to different types of self-inflicted harm. For example, compare the conventional nursing approach to stigmatised conditions and presentations such as Scarlet's self-harming to the approach taken to sports injuries and infected piercings. While all such injuries, and many more, may arise directly or indirectly from the personal choices of individuals, some injuries are seen as shameful while others are considered almost heroic! Sometimes I think we need to have a serious think about why we are in nursing and what it is we want to achieve through our interactions and interventions.

I would like to see all nurses equipped with the knowledge and skills needed to practise in trauma-informed ways, whatever the setting. Current service pressures can mean that patients like Scarlet are not always (or not generally) getting their needs met. Yet a shift in understanding about the legitimate needs of people who have sometimes experienced multiple adverse childhood events leading to coping strategies which are not properly understood by those around them could make a life-changing difference to people like Scarlet. Now that is why I am glad I am a nurse, and why my role is so worthwhile. Challenging though it is, it will keep getting me out of bed in the morning. The Scarlets of this world need nurses like me, nurses who recognise her as a person who is worth taking the time to understand better.

Questions for reflection and discussion

1. Where do views on the 'deserving patient' come from and how can you challenge such perceptions?

2. Should there be limits on compassion where people are self-harming? Why do you think this?

3. What types of cognitive bias might come into play for you and other members of your team when working with people who have self-harmed?

4. How can you and your team best support one another to be understanding towards each other, and towards patients whose actions can seem both problematic and difficult to understand?

5. What steps can you and your team take towards providing 'trauma-informed' services in all health and social care settings?

6. In what ways might working with patients like Scarlet challenge your assumptions about the diverse roles of nurses and the purposes of healthcare services?

Further information

VALUES

Patient-centred care Requires a therapeutic relationship between the professional and service user that is unattainable when the service user is thought of as a diagnosis, presenting problem or cubicle number. Built on effective communication, it has service users' needs, values and choices central to the development of care plans and care delivery (Gluyas, 2015).

Communication This is *'central to successful caring relationships and to effective team working. Listening is as important as what we say and do'* (Department of Health, 2012, p 13). Communication in nursing practice is central to all aspects of the nursing process (Kourkouta and Papathanasiou, 2014).

Efficient and effective care Achieving the delivery of efficient and effective care in nursing is part of improving the quality-of-service delivery and is underpinned by the Royal College of Nursing's (2010) Principles of Nursing Practice.

Judgements and assumptions Making premature judgements and assumptions can impact the decision-making process in nursing, affecting future actions and care planning in detrimental ways (Nibbelink and Brewer, 2018).

Empathy and compassion Empathy in nursing practice is the ability to put yourself in the patient's shoes and understand the world from their perspective (for further information, see Moudatsou et al, 2020). Compassion is defined in *Compassion in Practice* as *'how care is given through relationships based on empathy, respect and dignity'* (Department of Health, 2012, p 13).

'Hello, my name is' campaign Dr Kate Granger, a medical doctor living with a terminal illness, began the 'Hello, my name is' campaign with her husband in 2013 to encourage and remind healthcare staff about the importance of introductions in healthcare. Further information is available on the campaign website: www.hellomynameis.org.uk

Non-judgemental The 2018 Standards for Competence for Registered Nurses state that all nurses' practice should be non-judgemental, holistic, caring and sensitive (NMC, 2018b).

Professionalism The NMC (2018b) describe professionalism as being characterised by *'autonomous evidence-based decision making by members of an occupation who share the same values and education'*, expressing the understanding that in nursing this leads to *'the consistent provision of safe, effective, person-centred outcomes that support people and their families and carers, to achieve an optimal status of health and well-being'*.

Unconditional positive regard A key aspect of person-centred theory as proposed and practised by Carl Rogers (in Suhd, 1995), who stated that positive regard enables our service users to feel respected and valued within the therapeutic relationship. He considered that every individual develops a view of themselves which arises from interacting with people who play important roles in their childhoods. If people experience being loved, valued and respected, they feel worthy of love, value and respect (see Chapman, 2017 for further information on utilising person-centred care in contemporary nursing practice).

Acceptance Just like non-judgemental approaches to care and offering unconditional positive regard, acceptance is a key value which promotes person-centred practice in nursing. See McCormack et al (2021) for further information on person-centred practice in nursing and healthcare.

Courage *Compassion in Practice* notes that: *'Courage enables us to do the right thing for the people we care for, to speak up when we have concerns and to have the personal strength and vision to innovate and to embrace new ways of working'* (Department of Health, 2012, p 13).

Patient empowerment The World Health Organization describes patient empowerment as a journey rather than a destination: *'empowerment refers to the level of choice, influence and control that users of mental health services can exercise over events in their lives. The key to empowerment is the removal of formal or informal barriers and the transformation of power relations'* (WHO, 2010, pp 1–2).

Competence *Compassion in Practice* (Department of Health, 2012, p 13) describes competence as incorporating *'the ability to understand an individual's health and social needs and the expertise, clinical and technical knowledge to deliver effective care and treatments based on research and evidence'*.

Caring The Code (NMC, 2018b) states that nursing care should be patient centred and it provides guidance on 'caring with confidence'.

Record keeping Accurate record keeping is both a legal requirement and a standard of best practice.

THEORIES

Transitions in care NICE (2016) published guideline NG43 to outline best practice for supporting the transition from children's to adults' services. NHS trusts often supplement this with their own policies and procedures outlining the steps that should be taken, including planning, communication and periods of transition where both services are involved. However, due to resources, transition processes are often triggered by admin and service users find themselves moved from one team to another without adequate time to build therapeutic relationships with new caregivers, or to have therapeutic endings with old caregivers, leading to distress.

Active listening This is an essential aspect of respecting the patients with whom we interact. Becoming an effective listener involves actively engaging with people to make sense of what we see in their body language, in combination with what we hear. We need to hear, consider and process what is said to us in nursing, and this can never be a passive process (Ali, 2018).

Revolving door syndrome The Center for Disease Control and Prevention (2020) state that the revolving door syndrome whereby crisis episodes repeat is due to early discharge and poor community follow-up. While the UK does not currently have insurance-driving pressures for early discharge as suggested by the CDC, bed shortages and a shortage of resources mean that interactions can be shorter than ideally necessary and less therapeutic.

Therapeutic relationships Optimal relationships within healthcare are generally identified as being therapeutic to patients due to being a key aspect of providing care and acting as a potential catalyst to recovery. For a more detailed understanding of therapeutic relationships in nursing, see Wright (2021).

Organisational cultures Recognising and actively working on organisational cultures is important, with the Francis Report highlighting the negative impact of poor organisational cultures (Powell, 2013).

Self-harm Deliberate self-harm is recognised as a means of managing mental and emotional distress through the intentional injuring of oneself without suicidal intent. Klonsky et al (2003) found that about one of every 25 members of a large group of relatively high-functioning non-clinical subjects reported a history of self-harm. Those who self-harmed tended to have more symptoms of several personality disorders than those who did not. Their performance across measures suggested that anxiety plays a prominent role in their psychopathology.

Cognitive dissonance This theory postulates that an underlying psychological tension is created when an individual's behaviour is inconsistent with their thoughts and beliefs. This underlying tension then motivates an individual to make an attitude change that would produce consistency between their thoughts and behaviours. Cognitive dissonance theory was originally proposed by Leon Festinger in 1957.

Burnout Refers to a state of emotional exhaustion, depersonalisation and reduced accomplishment in work-related tasks, often arising from an excessive workload (Maslach, 1999). Many research studies have provided evidence on the negative impact of burnout, which has been linked to *reduced patient safety and adverse events, including medication errors, infections and falls* leading to increases in: *patient dissatisfaction and family complaints* (Dall'Ora and Saville, 2021, p 44). Mudallal et al (2017, p 1) identified ways in which *burnout lowers nurses' quality of life, performance level, and organisational commitment and increases their intention to leave the job*.

Adverse childhood experiences (ACEs) These are traditionally understood as a set of ten traumatic events or circumstances occurring before the age of 18 that have been shown through research to increase the risk of adult mental health problems and debilitating diseases. Five ACE categories are forms of child abuse and neglect, which are known to harm children and are punishable by law, and five represent forms of family dysfunction that increase children's exposure to trauma (Asmussen et al, 2020, p 6). See Early Intervention Foundation (2020) for more information.

Coping mechanisms For an interesting discussion on the differences and similarities between coping mechanisms and emotional regulation, see Compas et al (2014). Coping mechanisms involve using strategies as a way of managing painful or difficult emotions arising from stress or trauma and can help in adjusting to stressful events in a way which contributes to maintaining well-being in the face of such events. However, some people will use coping mechanisms which are considered to be maladaptive as they cause harm. These include the use of alcohol or other mind-altering substances, as well as other forms of self-injury.

Emotional overwhelm An emotionally overwhelmed person is likely to be experiencing intense emotions which are difficult to manage, affecting their control of both internal thoughts and external actions or behaviours. Emotional overwhelm may be caused by a wide range of situations contributing to an inability to process feelings as they arise. A person experiencing many conflicting feelings simultaneously is especially likely to become emotionally overwhelmed.

Attachment, separation John Bowlby used the term *maternal deprivation* to refer to separation from, or loss of, an attachment figure, as well as the inability or lack of opportunity to develop an attachment to any person (Bowlby, 1968). People who experience separations from their parents as children may experience low self-esteem, a general distrust of others, mood disorders (including depression and anxiety) and difficulty coping with situations provoking strong emotions in adult life.

Emotional regulation This refers to the ability to effectively exert control over one's emotions through a wide range of strategies used to influence which emotions are experienced or expressed (Gross, 2020). See Dunkley (2020) for further information on emotional regulation using DBT.

Socialisation The process an individual undergoes to learn values, norms and customs in accordance with the societal needs and expectations of the society within which they live.

Compliance with social norms Social norms arise from the beliefs, attitudes and behaviours that are considered acceptable in a particular social group or culture, providing an idea of how to behave in a range of social situations and therefore leading to greater order and a certain amount of predictability in society and social relationships. Most people usually experience considerable social pressure to conform to the prevailing norms in any given situation.

Loss and the grief response Grief is a response to loss of any kind and does not necessarily involve the death of a person close to us: it can also arise as a result of losing contact with an important person, loss of an object, end of the stage of one's life or other significant change. The grief experience has been described as involving five stages of processing the loss (Kubler-Ross and Kessler, 2014).

Emotional dysregulation Fitzpatrick et al (2020) describe emotional dysregulation as involving lower basal vagal tone, higher baseline emotion, heightened emotional reactivity, delayed emotional recovery and emotion regulation deficits.

Self-injury and self-help versus future risk In making an assessment of the risks associated with self-harm, it is important to recognise that for some people this can be a sign of ongoing hope (Motz, 2010), yet for others non-suicidal self-injury can be a risk factor for future completed suicide (Hamza et al, 2012).

Risk management/safety planning Higgins et al (2015, p 13) suggest that: '*A safety plan should aim to capture a summary of the risk identified, formulations of the situations in which identified risks may occur, including warning signs, factors that may escalate the risk and strategies to be taken by practitioners and the service user in response to risks identified. The strategies identified should be aimed at: promoting positive or therapeutic risk taking, preventing negative events from occurring or, if this is not possible, minimising the harm caused.*'

Self-harm as emotional regulation In a discussion on self-injury in the regulation of emotion, Andover and Morris (2014) note that non-suicidal self-injury is often carried out as a strategy for regulating emotions as it can decrease the experience and intensity of negative feelings.

Social stigma This type of stigma, along with discrimination, can delay recovery from mental ill health and add to the experience of mental distress (Mental Health Foundation, 2021).

Self-soothing Examples of approaches to self-soothing to increase tolerance of distressing emotions and to support self-management of emotions in a positive way are provided by McKay et al (2019).

Parasympathetic nervous system Linehan (2015, p 340) in noting that emotions involve changes in the nervous system, describes how the sympathetic and parasympathetic nervous systems complement each other in activating and deactivating the stress response.

Dialectics Linehan (1993) explains that dialectics is the balance between change and acceptance. Change can only occur if one accepts what is.

APPROACHES

Trauma-informed care Trauma symptoms are recognised and the role trauma can play in an individual's life – including in the lives of nurses – is acknowledged. Adopting this approach has the potential to improve patient engagement, treatment adherence and health outcomes, as well as staff wellness.

History taking Accurate history taking is a key aspect of nursing assessment, ultimately leading to improved care planning and patient outcomes (Fawcett and Rhynas, 2012).

Multidisciplinary team working Multidisciplinary teams play an essential role in providing holistic care to patients, as nurses, occupational therapists, social workers, psychiatrists, psychologists and clinical support workers work together to provide holistic care.

Working with looked after children A child who has been in the care of the local authority for more than 24 hours is known as a looked after child. Looked after children may also be referred to as children in care, with some children and young people preferring the latter term. There is evidence from some research studies suggesting that when looked after children are compared with children who have not been in care, they are likely to have poorer outcomes in educational achievement, as well as in mental and physical health (Rahilly and Hendry, 2014).

Validation This involves acknowledging the validity in what someone else is thinking, feeling or doing without the need to understand, agree with or condone these behaviours. Balancing validation (acceptance strategies) and problem-solving (change strategies) forms the core of DBT (Linehan, 1993).

Health education This consists of providing opportunities for learning involving developing understanding and knowledge which lead to health improvements. However, health education is not only concerned with the communication of information but also with developing motivation and a sense of self-efficacy which increase the likelihood of changes taking place that will improve health.

Dialectical behaviour therapy (DBT) This is a psychotherapeutic approach originally designed and proposed by Marsha Linehan (1987) as a way of supporting people with suicidal ideation and self-harming behaviours arising from emotional dysregulation to manage and process their feelings. DBT has been adapted to successfully treat emotionally unstable personality disorders. See Dunkley (2020) for contemporary guidance on this approach.

Positive risk taking The desired outcome of positive risk taking is to encourage and support people to achieve personal change and the development of enhanced well-being. It does not mean trying to eliminate risk but is a way of managing risks to maximise people's choice and control over their lives. Positive risk taking recognises that in addition to potentially negative characteristics, risk taking can have positive benefits for individuals, enabling them to do things that promote well-being. A balance has to be achieved between the wishes of adults at risk of self-harm and the nurse's duty of care. See Hart (2014) for further guidance on risk assessment and management in mental health.

Risk assessment Involving Scarlet in the assessment of her own safety is a key component of empowering her to make decisions which promote her well-being. However, care needs to be taken to ensure that patients are not left feeling that they are completely on their own and without much-needed support. Risk management therefore also includes developing a safety plan with the patient. See Higgins et al (2015) for further information.

Recognising the need for support for unpaid carers See Hall and Melia (2022) for an example of research exploring the approach taken by friends supporting young people who self-harm.

Distraction Dunkley (2020, p 6) explains how the pain resulting from self-harm can distract the person in distress from experiencing emotions which feel out of control. However, distraction as a therapeutic technique is seen as superficial, offering short-term benefit and not addressing the causes of the overwhelming emotions (Dunkley, 2020, p 81).

Patient safety The Code presents the professional standards that nurses, midwives and nursing associates must uphold to be registered to practise in the UK. It is structured around four themes which include preserving safety (NMC, 2018b, pp 13–17).

Harm-minimisation For examples of harm minimisation in self-harm, see Self-injury Support (nd).

Reflective practice The NMC require reflections as part of the revalidation requirements, and many teams conduct monthly reflective practice groups as important learning tools.

Self-care This is often neglected in today's busy schedules but is important for the maintenance of the mind and body.

MODELS

Prevention In 2020, the World Health Organization published a white paper outlining their evidence-based vision for promotive and preventive mental health interventions for adolescents (WHO, 2020).

Care-coordination This refers to the co-ordination of care through multidisciplinary teams across multiple care contexts. For more information, see Kuiper (2016).

The Medical Model A reductionist approach to healthcare practice which considers that illness is best diagnosed using systematic observations and descriptions which align with standard guidelines and procedures, such as specific tests and the description of symptoms (see Farre and Rapley, 2017, for further information).

Social and emotional development Silvers (2022) describes how parents who provide the scaffolding for emotional regulation during childhood gradually remove their support during adolescence, making social and emotional development during the teenage years key contributors to the subsequent ability to regulate emotions in healthy ways.

Behaviourism This is a psychological theory of learning which suggests that people learn behaviours through a process of conditioning by interacting with their environment. In relation to Scarlet's experience, she interprets the removal of care as being a form of punishment, which has the purpose of controlling her behaviour in specific ways by influencing her views of good and wrong ways to react – with 'good' behaviours being rewarded with attention and support, and those perceived as being 'wrong' as leading to the withdrawal of that support and care. Behaviourism was a commonly used approach in care settings in the past, and pockets of behavioural practice continue to exist in contemporary health and social care.

Biosocial model DBT's biosocial model is a transactional theory which considers that inborn emotional sensitivity combined with an invalidating environment (for example, a family context in which the person's feelings are not understood) lead to emotional dysregulation (see Linehan, 1987 and Dunkley, 2020 for further information).

Clinical supervision Used to support the provision of better-quality care to patients. This is achieved through discussions which support practice development by helping nurses to reflect on their decision making and actions taken as well as potential strategies for future practice.

MDT working Multidisciplinary team working involves more than working alongside health practitioners from other professions or nurses at a different stage of their career. It also provides opportunities for taking into consideration different professional perspectives of relevance to decision making, positive risk taking and reflection on and in practice. Ultimately, these different perspectives can potentially lead to better patient outcomes.

Biomedical model The main model used in Western healthcare, where in the absence of disease or illness there is health. Thompson (2018, p 11) describes approaches to understanding mental distress as being socially constructed – suggesting that it is a product of *'social forces that change as society changes on its path through history'*. In this sense, the biomedical model is seen as no longer having relevance as the main model to draw upon in understanding the origins of mental distress.

Further reading

Delves-Yates, C (2021) *Beginner's Guide to Reflective Practice in Nursing*. London: Sage Publications.

Dunkley, C (2020) *Regulating Emotion the DBT Way: A Therapist's Guide to Opposite Action*. Abingdon and New York: Routledge.

Homes, A and Grandison, G (2021) *Trauma-Informed Practice: Toolkit*. NHS Scotland in partnership with NHS Education for Scotland. [online] Available at: www.gov.scot/publications/trauma-informed-practice-toolkit-scotland/documents (accessed 23 February 2023).

McCormack, B (2021) *Fundamentals of Person-Centred Healthcare Practice: A Guide for Healthcare Students*. Hoboken, NJ: Wiley-Blackwell.

Nock, M K (2017) *The Oxford Handbook of Suicide and Self-Injury*. Oxford: Oxford University Press.

Part 3

Personalising care

Case study 11
Stephanie: see me, hear me, include me

Sally Hardy

I was asked to meet a young woman called Stephanie in my capacity as community mental health nurse by the general practice administrator. This was as a follow-up to a consultation Stephanie had with her GP the week before. During the GP consultation, Stephanie had presented as being highly agitated and exhibited repetitive picking behaviours around her nail beds that had caused them to bleed during the appointment. Stephanie had been given a prescription for anxiety and some sleeping tablets, but the GP wanted to explore if anything more could be done to help with the behavioural issue of skin picking.

APPROACH: history taking

I tried telephoning the number on file for Stephanie, but there was no answer. I decided to both text and post a formal appointment letter to ensure I had used all forms available for making initial contact with her. The date and time of the appointment came, and I was still not certain if I had managed to make contact. However, in walked a young woman, dressed in a hijab. She was tall, slim built and dressed all in black. I checked the medical notes and her date of birth indicated she was 19 years old. I smiled and welcomed her into the consulting room, where she sat on the chair beside the desk with her head bowed, gently rocking her body backwards and forwards. I noticed she was wearing black gloves, long black jeans and lace-up boots so only the skin on her face was visible. She was, however, wearing make-up.

APPROACH: communication

MODEL: multicultural society

THEORY: adolescent mental health

APPROACH: observational assessment

'Hi, my name's Sally, I am pleased to meet with you today. How can I help you?' She glanced up at me, and there were tears in her eyes. I leant forward slowly and said, '*Tell me what is happening?*'

She let out a soft groan and the rocking motion got faster. '*You are safe here; it is only you and me in the room. What can I call you? Stephanie, or do you prefer Steph?*' I enquired, trying to establish a rapport to enable her to speak freely. She was so tense; it was beginning to make me feel tense and anxious. We

VALUES: person-centred practice; self-reflection

THEORY: transference

MODEL: counselling

THEORY: psychodynamic
psychotherapy

APPROACHES: safety procedures
at work; observational
assessment

APPROACH: clarification
questions

VALUE: cultural awareness

APPROACH: cultural
competencies

APPROACH: psychodynamic
principles

sat in silence for what felt like ages but was probably only a minute. I held her eye contact, still leaning forward towards her to offer some reassurance I was not going anywhere.

Stephanie kept up the rocking motion but slowly lifted her gaze. It felt like she was checking me out to see if I was telling her the truth. '*I can see you are upset; what is it that is upsetting you*?' I asked.

She glanced at the door. I wondered if she was going to flee the room as her chair was right next to the door, and my desk was beside the wall. I was hemmed in, but reassuringly felt the alarm under the office desk, which I could readily hit with my knee to call and alert the office staff if necessary. I also had time to notice some scratches on her cheeks, just visible under the make-up and her hijab.

Stephanie whispered, '*I can't, it will make him angry*'.

'*Who will be angry?*'

'*My uncle*', she replied softly, glancing again at the door.

'*Your uncle will be angry with you for coming to the doctors?*' I replied.

'*He will think I am getting contraception, or being seen by a man; this is not good for me.*'

'*How can I help you and reassure your uncle that coming here is important for your health and well-being?*'

'*I don't know what to do.*' She was now on the edge of her chair and had pulled off one of the gloves to start picking at her finger-nail. It was red, angry and sore looking. An external cue to what she was feeling on the inside, I thought to myself.

'*Can I ask what the scratches are on your face?*' I replied, probing further to understand the situation for this young woman. Stephanie flashed a glance at me, as if in disbelief.

'*I have to keep clean. Keep the house clean. I am a burden to my family. I cannot get a job, but if I get a job, I have to leave the house, and he will get angry.*' At this point she was fully sobbing.

I found her a tissue on my desk. When I stretched out my hand to offer the tissue, she recoiled.

MODEL: domestic/sexual abuse

'*Does your uncle hurt you Steph?*' I asked directly, trying to get to the issue at hand so that I could then decide what the next steps needed to be.

MODEL: safeguarding

'*How do you know?*' she asked, as if I had somehow seen inside her world with that one question.

'*I can see your scratches. You are incredibly nervous, rocking in your chair, and you are getting upset talking to me; you appear scared and at a loss. I need to see your arms as well please Stephanie. Are you hurting yourself anywhere else? I can help you, but you need to tell me more about what is happening at home. Can you do that?*'

MODEL: self-harm

She looked again at the door. '*Did your uncle come with you today; is he outside?*'

She nodded as if not wanting anyone to hear her response. '*Okay, here is what we can do. I will call my colleague Jayne on reception and she can see where your uncle is, and we can also get someone to speak with him.*'

'*No, please no, that will not help me*', she pleaded.

'*Okay, so what will help you?*' I asked.

'*I need more tablets to help me sleep, help me forget.*' Stephanie was looking at the floor again, still rocking. She lifted the sleeves of her jumper to reveal a series of scratches and lines criss-crossing her forearms.

'*Are you using the tablets for yourself?*' I asked, as I was aware she had just last week been given a prescription. '*My mother, she needs to sleep. She watches me, and she gets in the way. He hits her, and then comes for me in the night. He wants to look after me, and he wants to take me away. It is his duty to look after me and my mother. He tells me things I cannot tell anyone else. I don't know what to do, and when I try to go out, he follows me and so it goes on, on on… I can't tell my friends, and I can't bring them home anymore; he will try to get them to do the same as me, I know it.*'

Reflections

The case with Stephanie was a particularly memorable one and set off a whole series of referrals, team conversations and inter-agency interventions to fully understand the extent of what was happening with Stephanie's family situation. It took a while to get Stephanie to talk and reveal some of her situation and story, which had been going on for many years before she had found the courage to attend the GP surgery and seek help. She was motivated by the desire to protect her mother rather than for her own safety, as her own sense of self-worth was at rock bottom. As the practitioner I had to remain calm and attentive, but not put pressure on her to then scare her off. I used skills of observation and questioning. When I asked about her scratches, this was the one question that triggered a change in her acceptance of me, and allowed Stephanie to recognise I was seeing her, as if for the first time. She told me afterwards that this was the first time she felt someone had noticed her and showed genuine interest to ask her about her situation, rather than wanting to get her to do something. She had also stopped eating and therefore her menstrual cycle had stopped. She was anorexic, not just slim, trying to remain in the shadows so no one would notice her.

This case reminded me how it is important to balance cultural context with health and safety interventions. While it was not in my or Stephanie's interest to make assumptions about her statement that her uncle was looking after them, she said herself that it is his duty to look after them. If her father was dead, or not in this country, then it would fall to the closest male in the family to offer protection and support. It was only when she said her mother was being hit, and her response to my offer of a tissue, where she recoiled, that I started to become aware of the potential level of abuse that might be happening in the home. Safeguarding cases are always complicated and can take a long time to proceed, following the legal pathways and procedures. We did manage to find Stephanie and her mother a women's refuge, and they are settled there, smiling and interacting with people more freely. Stephanie has started a degree in social work and is focusing on supporting refugees and asylum seekers – a cause close to her heart.

Questions for reflection and discussion

1. When assessing someone in a consultation, what can be done to maximise the opportunity in that short space of time available?

2. How can practitioners remain up to date in terms of the multicultural aspects of health and social care?

3. What strategies are useful when working with a person who is self-harming?

4. When a practitioner becomes suspicious of abuse or neglect, what are the procedures to follow to ascertain the right support and information needed to address this?

5. Who are the key agencies and personnel that need to be involved in safeguarding cases such as this one?

6. What does a practitioner need to do to keep themselves resilient to such cases as this, where the impact on the practitioner can also be long lasting?

Further information

VALUES

Person-centred practice Focusing attention on the person as a whole, not just their physical or mental state, is an important value-based approach to delivering care that is right for that person. Understanding the person is central to getting the care right for them and adapting approaches to suit their situation and preferences (McCormack and McCance, 2016). History taking, getting to know the person and their likes and dislikes, enables close relationships to form quite quickly between a patient and their carer, allowing that person to be heard, valued and accepted for who they are, unique in their own lives.

Self-reflection A process that can be used to increase reflective practice is doing a self-check by taking the time to assess and pay attention to any internal thoughts or feelings that are emerging as you assess the person. The ability to be self-aware is a crucial tool in therapeutic relationships based on psychodynamic principles of interacting meaningfully with people (Sherwood et al, 2022).

Cultural awareness Understanding what needs to be included in healthcare settings to improve cultural awareness, sensitives and practitioner competencies has been identified as key to ensuring high-quality access for diverse groups of people. Principles of cultural awareness can include cultural safety, humility and cultural intelligence, all of which provide the practitioner with a broad spectrum of knowledge from which to adapt their skills and accommodate the needs of the person. Having this level of awareness is considered best practice (Shepherd, 2019).

THEORIES

Adolescent mental health Being an adolescent is not necessarily defined by age, although for many it falls between 12 and 24 years. Puberty is often seen as a key indicator of the start of adolescence, whereas in some countries children are expected to move from childhood to adulthood from 13 years old. Some now argue that adolescence is an outdated concept and should be replaced with the term 'young person'. The risk factors and social pressures of young people are well recognised as affecting their mental health and well-being. Educational achievements, sexual health and awareness, and societal and family pressures can all influence a young person's sense of who they are and who they want to be (Kieling et al, 2011).

Transference In psychotherapy, the word transference is quite a complex phenomenon, used to understand how feelings, emotions and sensations can be redirected to another person as an unconscious mechanism for relieving the individual of their difficult or strong emotions, which are attributed as originally felt and left undealt with from early phases of their personality development (Bateman et al, 2010).

Psychodynamic psychotherapy This is an approach to understanding a person from across the lifespan through the different developmental stages of a person's life. It is based on Freud's psychoanalytic theories but has emerged as a person-centred approach to talking therapy, exploring disturbances in early relationships and helping the person adapt and adopt new patterns of behaviour to lead more fulfilling lives and relationships. Bateman et al (2010) offer a very practical guide to working with this approach.

APPROACHES

History taking Being able to take a history from a patient is a key skill and vital component of the assessment process. Practitioners are expected to have the skillset to interview a person to gather relevant knowledge about the person that will directly inform the identification of care priorities. Several pieces of a person's life are gathered, including what they have come to seek help with on that day, as well as their past medical history, family history and what medication they take, both prescribed and unprescribed (self-medication such as recreational drugs and alcohol intake). Their mental well-being, social history, occupation and sexual activity can also be covered, which need to be undertaken with sensitivity and an explanation as to why these questions are considered relevant (McKenna et al, 2011).

Communication Effective communication and working with others is an essential element of any healthcare setting and teamwork. Communication can affect patient safety, and when communication breaks down, this is often at the core of clinical incidents. Understanding the exchange of information between people, where and how this can be strengthened, and where and how it can break down are core components of effective and safe clinical practice (Jacobs, 2017).

Observational assessment Using the skills of observation to undertake an assessment helps to validate what you are seeing in front of you compared to what information you have and what the person is telling you. For example, it is well known that many people will not always tell the truth when they are fearful of being reprimanded or know that they are going against advice. Being able to observe a person and use this to help formulate an assessment is a skill aligned with counselling and behavioural therapy (Jacobs, 2017).

Safety procedures at work Promoting good practices to ensure staff as well as patients are safe in the healthcare setting is of paramount importance. This is of particular importance as many practitioners are left alone in the company of strangers, so the potential for identifying in advance mechanisms to improve safety precautions is a duty of care, set out by employers and the law (Christian et al, 2009). By duty of care, this means the statutory obligations that are needed to achieve accepted standards of professional practice. For nurses, this comes with the Nursing and Midwifery Council (NMC) regulations for registration (NMC, 2018b).

Clarification questions In order to fully understand someone or something, you need to ask questions to clarify the situation. By probing deeper into something, this allows a fuller picture to emerge of the influential factors. Used most frequently in a counselling or initial consultation process, probing questions when undertaken over a sustained period can feel intimidating or exposing for a vulnerable or anxious person, so the questioning style must be adapted to allow the conversation to be rich and obtain the information needed to make an informed judgement. John Heron's six categories of interventions is a useful tool to understand the types of questions required for different outcomes and intentions (Heron, 1976).

Cultural competencies These are an organisation's response to working and providing effective healthcare access to all the diverse communities and groups of people that make up our modern multicultural society. It requires principles of representation across staff diversity, effective staff training packages, access to interpreter services, and improving staff attitudes to inclusion, equality and diversity at all levels of service provision through, for example, addressing microaggressions and other institutional-level prejudices and bias (Alladin, 1998; Henderson et al, 2018).

Psychodynamic principles An approach to interacting with an individual, drawing upon theories of psychotherapy, counselling and developmental and humanistic psychology. The word 'Psyche' is the common thread that brings together psychology, psychotherapy and psychodynamic approaches, which from the original Greek translates into the English word for the mind. When used as a therapeutic tool, this approach stretches to also include not just what is going on in someone's mind, but how the person is behaving and speaking; the words they choose all have meaning in helping the therapist understand the whole person (Bateman et al, 2010).

MODELS

Multicultural society Living within a multicultural society offers the opportunity to seek inclusion of the different views and contributions of each cultural heritage to identify and sustain a respectful and vibrant community, where multiple traditions are seen to enrich and enliven society by encouraging diversity to co-exist rather than being seen as an issue of derision (Wilde, 2023).

Counselling This is a talking therapy approach to providing a person with professional help and guidance for resolving their personal problems (Alladin, 1998). One of the core components of all counselling relationships is establishing the boundaries of that relationship and building rapport between the two parties to ensure that the working relationship will remain therapeutic, helpful and separate from other relationships the person is seeking.

Domestic/sexual abuse It is widely acknowledged that domestic and sexual abuse is a significant problem, particularly for women and young girls. However, all employers have a duty of care under the Health and Safety at Work Act to ensure as far as is possible that the health, safety and welfare of their employers is being safeguarded, through creating and ensuring a safe workplace, and ensuring that support is available to support survivors, signposting and referring to appropriate services. Defining what domestic or sexual abuse is can include any incident of coercion, violence, threatening behaviour, and physical, psychological, sexual, financial or emotional abuse. Identifying and spotting signs of abuse can include having secrets, changes in behaviour, problems with concentrating and engaging with others, and associated physical signs such as bruising or soreness. It is known that nine out of ten children are known or related to their abuser. Guidance documents and websites, such as the Care and Statutory Guidance (2022) updates, are particularly useful references.

Safeguarding Many people, particularly children, young people and the elderly, can become vulnerable to incidents of abuse. The term safeguarding was introduced in the UK by a Labour government in 2011, in response to untoward child deaths where investigations into incidents identified considerable lack of engagement between agencies working together to protect the child, rather than simply investigating the circumstances. Copperman and Brown (2021) outline principles for managing safeguarding in health and social care.

Self-harm Self-harm describes behaviours that are associated with a person undertaking an act of deliberate harm to themselves, usually a sign of their distress and an attempt to cope with highly stressful or anxiety-provoking situations, feelings and thoughts. Models and approaches to help someone who is self-harming will depend on their situation but can be dealt with by first understanding their situation, what the self-harm is offering them in terms of a release of their feelings, and whether there is an underlying self-destructive motivation that may lead them to suicidal thoughts as an ultimate solution to their problems. There are many websites that can offer help but seeking professional help (through counselling, for example) is highly recommended when confronted with a patient you suspect or can observe is self-harming. Several online resources are available at the back of this book as additional or further resources, for example, via the Centre for Mental Health Law and Policy (cmhlp.org) or the Mind charity website.

Further reading

Jacobs, M (2017) *Psychodynamic Counselling in Action*. Oxford: Sage.

Mental Health Foundation (nd) Suicide Prevention. [online] Available at: www.mentalhealth.org.uk/our-work/public-engagement/suicide-prevention (accessed 23 January 2023).

Mind (nd) Supporting Someone Who Feels Suicidal. [online] Available at: www.mind.org.uk/information-support/helping-someone-else/supporting-someone-who-feels-suicidal/about-suicidal-feelings (accessed 23 January 2023).

National Institute of Mental Health (nd) Suicide Prevention. [online] Available at: www.nimh.nih.gov/health/topics/suicide-prevention (accessed 23 January 2023).

Patel, V, Flisher, A J, Hetrick, S and McGorry, P (2007) Mental Health of Young People: A Global Public-Health Challenge. *The Lancet*, 369 (9569): 1302–13.

Case study 12
Jamil: false hope?

Rebekah Hill

The respiratory outpatient clinic appointments are running late again! I know the familiar dread of being off late and having to cancel plans and apologise profusely to friends and family as, once again, I have let them down because of work commitments. I grab the notes for the next patient the consultant and I are due to see, Jamil, and quickly scan them to bring myself up to speed with what to expect next.

Jamil is 46 years old and is about to be told he has a diagnosis of terminal lung cancer; he is a police officer in a busy urban catchment area. Jamil lives with his long-term partner and together they have two daughters, aged 11 and 9. As I look back on his notes, I discover that for months prior to the diagnosis being made, Jamil had noticed a dull ache in the side of his chest; he said it felt like it was in his ribs but had discounted it as being nothing to worry about. The ache gradually got worse to the point that Jamil was noticing it most of the time, and so he had gone to his general practitioner (GP) to get it checked out. Jamil's GP arranged a chest X-ray; it was not thought to be urgent, and so had taken six weeks to have the X-ray and get the report back (the NHS have a two-week wait time for any suspected cancers to be investigated (NICE, 2020), but Jamil was not thought to necessitate this).

> **APPROACH:** *patient-centred care*

> **THEORY:** *cancer prevalence and risk perception*

I knew from my experience as a nurse that the initial investigation for possible lung cancer is a chest X-ray; we have many patients attend outpatients with such a suspicion. The recommendations we use for caring for patients with possible lung cancer are the Suspected Cancer: Recognition and Referral guideline published in 2020. Although they advise an urgent chest X-ray for anyone who has haemoptysis, or has ever smoked and had a cough, chest pain, dyspnoea, weight loss, fatigue or appetite loss, Jamil had none of these, so was not triaged as needing an urgent X-ray. Some chest X-rays in patients with lung cancer are normal, so, for safety netting, a CT scan will be requested (chest X-rays cannot give a definitive diagnosis because they often cannot distinguish between cancer and other conditions, such as a lung abscess).

> **THEORY:** *cancer prevalence and risk perception*

Jamil's chest X-ray had shown a vague shadowing, which was thought to be due to an infection, although Jamil had no symptoms other than feeling a little lethargic. Jamil had been put on a week's course of antibiotics and a repeat chest X-ray had been requested. The second chest X-ray had also shown the vague shadowing, so more investigations were ordered. A chest CT scan had been completed, following which a bronchoscopy was undertaken and biopsies performed.

After four months of investigations, Jamil is finally about to be given the diagnosis of end-stage lung cancer with widespread bone metastases. This is when I first met Jamil and his partner, Jess, when he came in to receive his diagnosis in the outpatients' department. Although I had been in the case conference along with the respiratory physician, oncologist and numerous other clinicians where we discussed Jamil's history, the case was brought to life when I came face to face with the owner of the pathology report.

VALUE: communication

Jamil and Jess are sitting in the consultation room when we arrive; the consultant and I are based in an office in between two consultation rooms, which we flip between, alternating between patients to maximise the flow of patients through outpatients. The chairs are positioned so that we are all sitting in a circle, with the desk to one side, to improve the intimacy of the consultation.

APPROACH: patient-centred care

The consultant uses a model to structure their communication with Jamil, a model which is all too familiar to me now, having witnessed them breaking bad news many times. The SPIKES model facilitates the telling of a story of how we reached the point we are at today. SPIKES is an acronym for a communication framework we often use in oncology for breaking bad news to patients with cancer; it stands for **S**etting up, **P**erception, **I**nvitation, **K**nowledge, **E**motion, **S**trategy. The setting up allows planning of what must be said and, in a private setting, perception is when we enquire about the patient's understanding of what is happening. Invitation invites the patient to ask what they would like to know; knowledge provides information in small pieces; emotion ensures the feelings of the patient are recognised and empathised with; while strategy allows us to set out the medical plan of action (Baile et al, 2000). The consultant walks Jamil and Jess through the journey leading to the destination we have reached today – a devastating cancer diagnosis. The consultant has other patients to see, so must leave. I cannot

MODEL: SPIKES

THEORY: communication

imagine how they are feeling right now, having dealt the blow of cancer and then having to compose themselves to see yet more patients in a busy outpatients' clinic.

Jamil, Jess and I are left in the room when the consultant leaves. Jamil looks stunned by the news; Jess is by his side, and both are in silence and looking down. Jamil eventually says: *'No one had fired a warning shot; I didn't know it might be cancer, I don't even smoke or anything.'* Jamil explains that he is an ex-smoker, a social footballer and keen golfer. Risk factors can make you more likely to develop lung cancer. Smoking is by far the leading risk factor for lung cancer: around 80 per cent of lung cancers are caused by smoking according to Cancer Research UK, and one in 13 males and one in 15 UK females will be diagnosed with lung cancer in their lifetime. Jamil, having given up smoking a decade ago, may not perceive himself to be at risk; as such, the diagnosis is incongruent with his current healthy lifestyle, making it difficult for him to accept.

Jamil sits is silence for a while: *'Would you like some time alone?'* I ask Jamil and Jess. Jamil looks up, *'Yes please'*, he replies. I leave Jamil and Jess for 15 minutes; I collect some glasses of water and tissues before returning into the room. I gently knock on the door before entering, not wanting to invade their privacy. *'It's only me'*, I call out before entering, having heard Jamil call out *'It's okay to come in'*. Jamil and Jess have red bloodshot eyes; they have clearly both been crying and are sitting in chairs next to each other, holding hands. The diagnosis is clearly devastating to both Jamil and his partner, and we spend the next half an hour in the outpatients' department, during which Jamil goes through phases of talking, crying, composure and then talking again.

My earlier frustration of being late off pales into insignificance as I see the devastation of the diagnosis on Jamil and Jess. We have blown their world apart. So what if I am a little late? – at least I am going home to my family, and they are well.

I am conscious of Jamil's reaction. I know emotions are raw and can change quickly at this time; it is possible to react with anger or to cry – no two situations are the same. It is thought that we pass through five stages of bereavement – five emotional responses to grief: denial, anger, bargaining, depression and acceptance (Kuber-Ross, 2014). Grief can be caused by many situations, such as ending relationships, divorce, death, receiving terminal illness news or grieving a pending death. The stages are not linear, and people may not move through stages 1–5. Although there is no empirical evidence of the existence of the five stages, it is generally accepted that differing states of grief exist.

Jamil asks, *'What will happen now?'* Although the consultant had already explained, I go through the plan of care again. I explain to Jamil that his plan of care is a palliative treatment plan, designed to extend the length of his life and not to cure the cancer. After a long pause I ask Jamil, *'What are your thoughts now?'* He replies,

'Do you mean physically or mentally'. *'Let's try both'*, I answer. After a long silence Jamil starts to talk; his top lip quivers and he has glassy tear-filled eyes as he explains he feels like he is *'struggling'*. Mindful that Jamil had only just received his diag-

nosis, one would expect such a reaction. After another long pause I ask, *'Tell me more about the struggle'*. Jamil looks up and

says *'I feel like there is a black cloud over me, like an impending sense of doom'*. He explains that he understands he has cancer but fears living with the *'uncertainty of knowing if he is getting*

worse day by day or hour by hour, like, when will my time be up...'. Jamil continues, *'This situation feels intolerable. Are there no certainties other than I won't get better?* I wait a while and then reply, *'I understand you want answers, about your condition, its progression and your future, but there are no certainties, Jamil'*.

Jamil explains that he feels he could come to terms with his condition, that he had terminal cancer, but he is struggling to cope with not knowing what his remaining life would be like. He says

that *'the uncertainty is the most difficult thing'*. Jamil explains, *'I know I have cancer; I know it can't be cured but I can't live my life*

waiting for the inevitable – to die. What kind of life will we all have – just waiting for me to die'. I maintain eye contact with

Jamil, gently nodding to show I am listening, and to try and show I understand what he is saying. Earlier in the consultation, when

the consultant asked Jamil if he wanted to talk about his prognosis, Jamil had shaken his head: *'No, no thank you, I don't want to know'*, he had replied. Jamil had continued, *'No one really knew for sure how long I've got, so I'd rather not have that conver-*

sation'. Yet not knowing was also posing a challenge for Jamil.

It is common to want some certainties about any situation that we are unsure about, and especially about health uncertainties – we want to know about a diagnosis, a prognosis, a disease trajectory; but often there are no fixed answers, no certainties.

Jamil's diagnosis had triggered a health transition. Transition in the context of this case relates to the process of a changed self-identity and the experience of uncertainty which relates to the ongoing consequences of living with a chronic condition, existing until a valued identity is achieved (Selder, 1989).

In chronic illnesses, most people gain a new perspective of living with the disease whereby they grow to develop a new appreciation of their life and identity with disease (Charmaz, 1991), while maintaining uncertainties about the disease. However, many people fail to make a healthy transition to life with illness and continue to live with elevated levels of sustained uncertainty, hoping for a cure. In this case, using what we know about chronic illness can be helpful with a cancer diagnosis – the transition and uncertainties can be the same. Uncertainty over time is harmful to quality of life. Studies show how the long-term consequences of sustained uncertainty of living with a chronic illness alter an individual's expectations of their future as well as their morale (Brown et al, 2020).

Sharing the experiences of others in similar situations and '*normalisation*' of feelings is known to be helpful for people with uncertainty (Mishel and Clayton, 2008), so I talk to Jamil about how many people with chronic illness have been known to experience 'uncertainty'. Uncertainty about their health, their daily lives, their roles, their finances, their illness. Jamil looks up and seems to take an interest in what I am saying; he gives me eye contact and stops crying, listening intently. I explain that chronic illness is anything that people are not cured of, that they live with. '*So, in a way, my cancer is like a chronic illness*', Jamil says. '*I'm not going to get better from it, but I could learn to live with it, like a chronic illness?*' From the moment Jamil poses the question, he seems to be lifted from a state of despair to one of hope. Jamil sits up straight, and then says he feels able to '*handle things better*' and even smiles.

For a moment, I feel uncomfortable; Jamil's shift in thinking seems immense, from doom and despair to a sense of stability and order. I feel guilty: have I done the right thing? Did I say the right thing? Feeling responsible for the transformation in Jamil's state of mind, was I wrong to compare his terminal diagnosis to a chronic illness; was I misleading him?

Yet the shift in framing Jamil's cancer from a terminal condition to a chronic illness seemed to give him hope. Hope might be seen from a positive standpoint of enabling someone to feel they have an influence on their situation, that they have some control (Snyder, 2002); such a perception is clearly enormously important to Jamil. Although Jamil could not change the inevitable outcome of his situation, he could have some autonomy over how he lived his life and perceived his condition. What worked for Jamil was to see his cancer as a chronic illness, something to live with, for now, rather than waiting to die from it.

Hope is known to reduce uncertainty, the feeling of loss of control. For Jamil it provided him with the important sense of self-rule. As a nurse, while I want to help Jamil cope with his diagnosis, I do not want to foster a sense of false hope, allowing him to think he might change the outcome of his situation. I walk a thin line with Jamil between hope, false hope and hopelessness.

Most people with chronic conditions hope one day to live without it. Lazarus (1999) states that hope is to believe something positive could materialise. The fundamental condition of this hope is that the current circumstance is unsatisfactory; they are concerned about what is going to happen and hope there will be a change for the better. Hope is a vital resource sustaining us since uncertainty underlies hope and hence hope is vital to cope against despair (hope to cope) (Lazarus, 1999). The uncertainties of not being able to predict a prognosis or determine the course of the illness are enduring and wearing in all chronic illnesses (Bury, 1982; Selder, 1989). Many people live in the hope that the situation will one day be resolved. The inability to forecast the disease equates to an inability to predict any future (Bury, 1982).

A lot of people feel sadness upon the realisation that life with chronic illness is not on the terms that had been hoped for (Charmaz, 1991), when they fail to return to a normal life. Hope is a predominant feature of life with chronic illness. It is fundamental to an ability to control and cope with chronic illness; the belief that the individual has the capacity to influence their health outcome. Jamil could not influence the outcome of his condition, but he could influence the life he led in the meantime.

For Jamil, he reached acceptance of his situation through hope – hope that he might be able to influence his situation. Acceptance equates to Jamil finding a way of accommodating the illness into his life by altering his performance and in doing so giving meaning to his life, despite harbouring some ongoing concerns about progressive health failure.

I feel emotionally exhausted. We have desolated a family's life in one short outpatients' clinic appointment. My only recompense is that we delivered the news in a crafted and compassionate manner – there is no doubt that Jamil and Jess will remember the conversation forever. My other thought as I pack my bag to eventually leave, with a heavy heart, is that I know we cannot always stop people from becoming ill, but we can influence how they live with their condition. What a responsibility.

Reflections

On reflection, Jamil should have been pre-warned about the possibility of a cancer diagnosis. At the point of investigation, patients often attend one appointment after another, and may not be seen by a health practitioner until all results are in, yet they are usually told what the investigations might reveal or what the suspicions are. I wonder if Jamil was told but did not recall this, discounting it as being a too remote possibility to be concerned with. Having given up smoking ten years previously, smoking was no longer part of Jamil's identity – hence compounding the shock of the diagnosis.

The communication model of SPIKES was useful in the setting of breaking bad news, yet ICE might have also really helped here (Pendleton et al, 2003). ICE is an acronym for Ideas, Concerns and Expectations. If we had started the consultation with ICE, we might have then discovered the extent to which Jamil had no expectation of the diagnosis.

I feel the framing of cancer into a chronic illness had helped Jamil. Hope is a powerful perception, without which there is hopelessness. I remain very aware of the responsibility that we must be honest with patients and always tell the truth, but to do so in a way that might not cause more harm. We walk a fine line.

1. In relation to cancer, where do our perceptions of risk come from?

2. What are the stages of bereavement? Do they occur for everyone in the same order and are they relevant here?

3. How can you help someone make a transition?

4. Is it possible to make a healthy transition to ill health?

5. What steps can you take to increase the perception of autonomy?

6. Is the use of hope to cope ethical? Do you think it is an acceptable strategy to use?

Further information

VALUES

Communication The NMC (2018a) stress the importance of a nurse's ability to communicate effectively, outlining competencies that must be met to register as a nurse. Effective communication is essential to build therapeutic relationships with patients. As noted by Delves-Yates (2021b), you can listen without caring but you cannot care without listening.

Promote autonomy In this context, this involves promoting the individual's ability to self-govern; their ability to make their own decisions. The NMC (2018b) stress that nurses must always promote the autonomy, rights and choices of people in their care.

THEORIES

Cancer prevalence and risk perception Perceived risk is an important subjective phenomenon relating to the judgement about susceptibility to disease. Risk perception is an essential component of health behaviour in cancer detection, diagnosis and treatment (Tilburt et al, 2011).

Communication The importance of effective communication should never be underestimated in this scenario. Effective communication is about more than just exchanging information; it is about understanding the emotion and intentions behind the information. Communication may be verbal or non-verbal. It is a professional requirement that nurses demonstrate effective communication skills since they are the foundation for building partnerships and therapeutic relationships (NMC, 2018b).

Bereavement stages Kubler- Ross developed the five stages of grief in her 1969 book, *On Death and Dying*. The stages are not linear but include denial, anger, bargaining, depression and acceptance.

Transition The theory of transition involves the movement from one state to another, yet transition in the context of this case relates to the process of a changed self-identity and the experience of uncertainty, which exists until a valued identity is achieved (Selder, 1989).

Uncertainty A health transition is triggered when a diagnosis is given, altering the person's identity until the diagnosis is incorporated into a new sense of self; during this time, uncertainty exists until the transition is complete. The uncertainties of not being able to predict a prognosis or determine the course of the illness is enduring and wearing for individuals (Selder, 1989).

Hope A sense of hope is associated with better physical health and health behaviour outcomes, as well as higher psychological well-being, lower psychological distress and better social well-being (Long et al, 2020).

Chronic illness The National Institute for Health and Care Excellence (NICE) consider a long-term condition as one that lasts a year or longer and impacts on a person's life; they provide guidance for multiple conditions (NICE, nd). We also use the term chronic illness interchangeably, which Bury (1982) refers to as a biographical disruption, prompting the individual to rethink their assumptions, self-concept and expectations for the future.

Acceptance Psychological acceptance is reached when an individual embraces a personal, often distressing, subjective experience and does so without defence or grudge. In health, we tend to think of acceptance as being the point at which a person has increased well-being, where they reconsider their values, priorities and meaning of their health condition and have a sense of development (Telford et al, 2006).

APPROACHES

Patient-centred care This is individualised care that is respectful and responsive to patient preference, needs and values. Patient-centred care ensures there is a partnership between the patient and the nurse. NHS England support healthcarers developing patient-centred care.

Care planning This starts with a conversation between the patient and the nurse about the impact a condition is having on their life. The nurse develops a plan of care based on four components – assessment of the patient, planning the care, implementation of the care and evaluation (Hill, 2021).

Active listening Active listening requires that you listen, understand, respond and reflect on what is being said, and retain the information. Active listening shows patients you are respectful of what they say and helps build trust (Delves-Yates, 2021b).

Validation Validation is an important communication strategy. To validate someone is to help them feel heard and supported by listening acknowledging and rephrasing what they have said.

Empowerment The NMC (2018b) encourage nurses to empower patients to give them a sense of control over their situation.

MODELS

SPIKES framework This is often used to break bad news. It is a helpful method for providing organised communication in a complex situation (Baile et al, 2000).

Further reading

Charmaz, K (1991) *Good Days, Bad Days: The Self in Chronic Illness and Time*. New Brunswick, NJ: Rutgers University Press.

Delves-Yates, C (2021) *Beginner's Guide to Reflective Practice in Nursing*. London: Sage Publications.

Mannix, K (2017) *With the End in Mind*. London: HarperCollins.

National Institute for Health and Care Excellence (NICE) (2019) *Improving Supportive and Palliative Care for Adults with Cancer*. [online] Available at: www.nice.org.uk/guidance/csg4 (accessed 23 February 2023).

NHS England (nd) Developing Patient Centred Care. [online] Available at: www.england.nhs.uk/integrated-care-pioneers/resources/patient-care (accessed 23 February 2023).

Watson, M (2020) *Oxford Handbook of Palliative Care*. Oxford: Oxford University Press.

Case study 13
Jessica: what matters most

Emma Harris

'*Am I going to die?*' asked 38-year-old Jessica. It was 4 am and Jessica had just been admitted to the ward with acute abdominal pain. '*Please make it stop! I can't stand this pain any longer*', she shouted to me as I rushed past her bed space. '*Sorry Jessica, I'm coming, I promise! Be with you in a moment!*' I replied as I headed off towards the sluice.

As I exited the sluice, a colleague stopped me in my tracks and asked me to assist them with a rapidly deteriorating patient. I felt trapped between a rock and hard place! I could hear Jessica was getting increasingly distressed and repeatedly calling out to staff. '*Please stop this pain! Stop all the damn noise.*' The background noise of the ward with intravenous pumps beeping, monitors sounding alarms and patients calling out in pain and discomfort were all having a detrimental impact on Jessica's ability to cope. I knew I urgently needed to speak to Jessica and listen to her concerns but had too many conflicting priorities to contend with that I really didn't know what to do first!

I decided my immediate priority must be to administer Jessica some analgesia and I told my colleague that I will assist them as soon as I can but, in the meantime can they see if anyone else is free. An hour after receiving the analgesia and anti-emetics, Jessica appeared more settled and I now had some time to talk to her about her earlier query when she asked if she was dying. I knew that talking about her fears may allow Jessica to relax and enable her to get some sleep and she appeared relieved to be able to speak to someone.

APPROACH: symptom management

VALUE: person-centred care

THEORY: therapeutic relationship

I sat next to Jessica's bed, so I appeared relaxed and unrushed. '*Jessica, please can you tell me how are you feeling?*' Jessica explained: '*Over the last few months, I have been feeling unwell and had no appetite; I've lost a lot of weight! I feel exhausted all the time and I have a pain in the upper right side of my body; it seems to radiate under and around my rib cage and sometimes to my shoulder. I saw my GP, and he felt that it was due to my hectic life, trying to balance everything from working hard and looking after my two young children Oliver, three, and Esme, four. He suggested I take some time off work and if I didn't feel any better over the next* month make another appointment to see him. *As my pain was getting so much worse, I decided enough is enough and came to the emergency department instead of waiting'.*

I wondered privately to myself what was going on. Years of experience working in acute medicine alerted me that the cause of these symptoms could be something serious and life limiting. The importance of early identification of Jessica's illness and disease trajectory was crucial, particularly if palliative care was needed in order to allow her time to plan and make decisions about treatment options. As the early shift arrived, I handed over the investigations that had been requested for Jessica and told her I would see her later in the week.

I met Jessica again two days later on a day shift; it was good to hear from the night staff that Jessica had undergone all her exploratory investigations (X-rays, bloods, CT and MRI scans). However, the results were not good. I think mainly because of her age I was shocked to hear that she had advanced pancreatic cancer with liver metastases. Similarly to when I last met Jessica, she was agitated and distressed. She called out to me: *'Emma, please help me, I cannot continue like this.'* I assessed her pain by using a visual analogue scale – I find the simplicity of this scale helpful. Jessica described her pain as 9 out of 10, with 10 being the worst possible pain and 0 being no pain. She stated that it was sharp and stabbing as she held her right upper quadrant area and showed how it radiated around to her back and shoulder and was worse when she leant forward. I thought from her description that the pain may have a neuropathic element to it and wondered if a neuropathic medication could be added to her current analgesic regime. Would a short course of steroids work? If it was inflammation then steroids could also help her appetite. I decided I needed to speak to the doctor as soon as possible about Jessica's symptom management.

'I am so sorry, Jessica, that we don't seem to have got to grips with your pain. Please let me see what analgesics I can administer now and I will call the doctor to review your pain relief.' Jessica sobbed, *'Emma, the news is not good'.* I reflected her words back, *'the news is not good?'* Between her sobs she was able to say that the doctors were going to speak to her and her husband this afternoon about her investigation results. I thought to myself that this *'heads up'* meant that the prognosis was bleak as this approach is often used when breaking bad news as a *'warning shot'.*

'*Emma, I really do not feel any better and to be honest with you, I am feeling worse.*' This was a clear cue to continue our discussion and an opportunity to ascertain her understanding, concerns and expectations. Jessica stated that she heard one of the nurses say the word cancer but was unsure if that was about her. '*Emma, will you be with me this afternoon please?*' '*Of course, I'll be there*', I answered. I felt worried and anxious for her and her family. How devastating this news was going to be for them. We had formed a good relationship and I would do whatever I could do to help support her.

At 13.45, Jessica's husband, James, arrived on the ward. I introduced myself: '*Hello James, my name is Emma. I have been looking after Jessica and she has asked me to join you both for the meeting at 14.00, is that okay?*'

'*Yes of course, Emma, thank you so much. I was hoping to get here earlier but I have just dropped the children off at a friend's; they seemed unsettled, so I stayed with them.*'

'*I will leave you to spend some time with Jessica, and I will collect you both in ten minutes. I have arranged a room just off the ward where we can have the meeting.*' This would allow privacy and reduce disturbance for the couple. I thought about the children, Oliver and Esme. I wondered what they have been told about why mummy is in hospital. This is such a sad situation; how are they and James going to cope and manage?

The consultant Dr Phillips arrived at 14.00 with his team and after we were seated and introductions had taken place, Dr Phillips opened the conversation: '*Jessica, please can tell me how you are feeling and how the last couple of days have been for you?*' Jessica replied with a clear explanation about how she felt her condition was getting worse as the symptoms she was experiencing seemed uncontrollable. Dr Philips' next question was '*What is your understanding so far about your illness?*' Jessica stated that '*I have had lots of tests to see what is causing my pain, weight loss and lethargy*'. Dr Phillips stated '*Have you thought of what may be happening?*' Jessica started crying and so did James. '*I have something terrible going on, like cancer.*' The room was quiet.

Dr Phillips confirmed Jessica's thinking: '*Jessica and James, I am so sorry to tell you that the CT, blood tests and MRI scan have unfortunately confirmed that you have cancer, an advanced pancreatic cancer with metastatic spread to your liver.*' The room was quiet again. I had a lump in my throat, and I tried so hard not to cry; how hard this devastating news must be for Jessica and James.

We allowed time for James and Jessica to think more about what had been said. After some time, James raised his head and said: *'This cannot be happening to Jessica; she can have treatment, can't she? Can't she be cured?'*

'I am sorry but the cancer cannot be cured. We can see what can be done by asking the oncologists to see Jessica; we are all here to support you and your family and to see what we can all do to help', Dr Phillips responded, allowing time for further questions. I felt reassured that Dr Phillips was breaking the bad news as his communication skills were excellent. He never seemed in a rush and always gives clear and honest news in a sensitive and empathetic way.

After the consultation, I spent time with Jessica and James to listen to any concerns before taking Jessica back to the ward. They shed many tears and displayed a range of emotions from shock and sadness to anger. James was distraught: *'I wish I had been more insistent about getting Jessica seen sooner; we may have been able to catch it earlier'*. Later in the shift, I worked with the couple to produce a plan of her wishes for her ongoing care and future management, which included referrals to the oncologist and the specialist palliative care team. I felt that with Jessica's poor prognosis, we needed to organise her end-of-life care to ensure these last few weeks focused on symptom control and quality of life for Jessica and her family. Later that day, we moved Jessica to a side room so James could stay overnight, and they could have some privacy at this emotional time. I was pleased when the long day ended; I felt exhausted and emotional – life is just not fair. I walked my dog later that evening so I could reflect on my shift; the fresh air really helped me to unwind. I knew it was important to look after my own mental and physical well-being.

My next shift was after the weekend and by this time the oncologist and specialist palliative team had been to see Jessica and provided clear and realistic information about treatment options and outcomes to match Jessica's own individual priorities and wishes. Jessica seemed pleased that I was on duty and keen to update me. *'I have been offered palliative chemotherapy if I want to have it. I don't think this will*

THEORIES: active listening; loss and the grief response

VALUE: communication

VALUE: professionalism

APPROACH: informed consent

VALUE: quality of life

APPROACH: multidisciplinary team working

VALUE: privacy and dignity

MODEL: reflection

THEORY: burnout

APPROACH: continuity of care

help me from what the cancer doctor said, but James is insisting that I have it. I want quality of life rather than a little longer; I do not want to spend the time I have left struggling with more symptoms. It is about having some quality time with my friends and family'.

VALUE: quality of life

'Emma, what would you do?' What a question! I was aware of the next steps but it is important to listen to what a person says for accuracy and confirmation of their understanding, thoughts and feelings about the situation. I had to support her but also be mindful of not influencing her decision-making processes, which would be based on personal preferences, beliefs and values. If I were in a similar situation, what would I do? I really do not know. We spent some time discussing the information she had received from the oncology team of the risks, benefits and all the possible consequences of different options.

VALUE: differential coping

MODEL: shared decision making

VALUE: informed choice

THEORY: ethical principles

Following our discussion, Jessica felt ready to tell James exactly how she felt and why she had made the decision not to have chemotherapy. Jessica seemed more relaxed, and her symptoms of pain and her appetite had improved due to pain control. Also, a short course of steroids prescribed by the oncologist appeared to be working already. Or was it because she felt fully informed of her condition and that her wishes had been listened to and addressed? It is so important to remember that addressing suffering involves taking care of issues beyond physical symptoms; it is about taking that holistic approach.

MODEL: analgesic ladder for cancer pain

THEORY: Charter for Planning Ahead

I suggested that Jessica may want to develop an advance care plan. This is a document where Jessica could write down her thoughts and wishes so that healthcare professionals and her family are aware of her wishes for her care and treatment in the event that she is unable to make decisions for herself. In her advance care plan Jessica made it clear she did not want to be resuscitated or admitted to hospital again. She agreed to discuss the anticipatory care planning process for an emergency care situation with the medical team. Jessica, supported by James, had had clear discussions about what treatment she did not want, which resulted in the arranging and completing of the following legally binding documents: a lasting power of attorney for health and care decisions so that decisions can be made for her on her behalf and an Advance Decision to Refuse Treatment document so that if she wanted to refuse life-sustaining treatment, this must be put in writing, signed and dated in the presence of a witness.

THEORY: advance care plan

THEORY: ReSPECT form

THEORY: advance directive

Jessica was discharged from hospital with support from the community specialist palliative care services and her GP, who would know what other services were available to support her and her family, physically, psychologically, socially, spiritually and financially if required in the future and following her death. Jessica came up to me with a hug and said *'Emma, a massive thank you; I could not have gone through this without you'*. She seemed determined to live as actively as possible for as long as possible.

James contacted the ward a month later to tell me Jessica had died peacefully at home with her family and friends around her. James and his children, Oliver and Esme, were receiving ongoing bereavement counselling from the psychological support services provided by the local specialist palliative care team. Caring for and supporting children during end-of-life care is an integral part of nursing but for the purpose of this case study the focus has been primarily on Jessica and James. For children and young adult support, there are number or resources; the key is to try and not exclude them from the situation and talk to them as open and honestly as possible using the language/words/terminology they understand so they can share their emotions. This can be done through activities such as art, play, photos, memory boxes and stories.

Reflections

As a mother, Jessica caused me to reflect on the fragility of life and how such an out of the blue diagnosis can have such a devastating impact on a family. As a nurse I felt in a very privileged position to be able to make a difference to her life, albeit at the end of life. Things that made Jessica's care difficult for me were the frantic pace we need to work at in the acute setting and how conflicting patient demands can add frustration to what is already a physically and emotionally demanding job. Despite this I felt able to provide continuity of care, which is of paramount importance, as it reduced Jessica's need to repeat her history and stories to others. The supportive team around me and the involvement of the multidisciplinary team were key to working in such a co-ordinated and collaborative way.

Early identification of an individual's illness and palliative diagnosis is important for forward planning and management of their personalised care so they have choices, and that the care is planned and implemented to meet 'what matters most' to them. Discussing this was key in supporting Jessica in her decision-making processes, allowing time for her wishes to be documented ready for when she was unable make a decision. Dame Cicely Saunders' quote always resonates with me in palliative care situations. *'You matter because you are, and you matter to the end of your life. We will do all we can, not only to help you die peacefully, but to also live until you die.'* In scenarios such as Jessica's we only get one chance to get it right and the dilemmas we encounter are likely to involve making difficult and emotionally challenging decisions. The importance of 'dying well' for me is a fundamental aspect of human dignity.

THEORY: total pain

Questions for reflection and discussion

1. Reflect on a time in clinical practice when you had dilemmas regarding how you could prioritise your work. What strategies worked well and why?

2. What do you consider are the barriers that may arise in acute primary/community care when looking after end-of-life patients? How would you manage these barriers?

3. When is the time to have serious illness conversations? And what skills would you use to deliver these tender conversations?

4. If a patient asks you to discuss euthanasia with them, what strategies would you use to support them?

5. When organising a discharge home for a patient with a poor prognosis, what would you include in the planning process?

6. In what ways can you effectively support your professional colleagues in highly demanding and stressful times in clinical practice?

Further information

VALUES

Person-centred care This approach is key when individuals are nearing the end of life to ensure that a patient's wishes are at the forefront of their care. There are four principles to person-centred care: treating people with dignity, respect, and compassion; offering co-ordinated care, support and treatment; offering personalised care; and helping people to recognise and build on their strengths to enable a better quality of life (Health Foundation, 2016).

Empathy and compassion This is the ability to understand and share the personal experiences and feelings which can foster a trusting connection. Compassion is a quality and skill used to demonstrate care through relationships based on empathy, respect and dignity. Both empathy and compassion are at the heart of the Code (NMC, 2018b), which states that nurses must *treat people with kindness, respect and compassion*.

'Hello, my name is' campaign This was founded by Dr Kate Granger when she was going through her cancer diagnosis and treatment. This initiative was designed to encourage healthcare staff to introduce themselves to their patients as the first step in establishing a vital human connection, helping patients to relax and building trust.

Communication This is essential to building therapeutic relationships with patients. As noted by Delves-Yates (2021b), you can listen without caring, but you cannot care without listening. The NMC (2018b) stress the importance of a nurse's ability to communicate effectively, outlining competencies that must be met to register as a nurse.

Professionalism Healthcare is delivered by teams of professionals who need to communicate well, respecting the principles of honesty, respect for others, confidentiality, and responsibility for their actions to promote patient safety (NMC, 2018b).

Quality of life This is defined by the World Health Organization (2012) as *individuals' perception of their position in life in the context of the culture and value systems in which they live, and in relation to their goals, expectations, standards and concerns*.

Privacy and dignity The concept of dignity has four defining attributes: respect, autonomy, empowerment and communication. Respect includes self-respect, respect for others, respect for peoples' privacy, confidentiality and self-belief and belief in others. This is essential to meet individuals needs and requirements in their healthcare (NMC, 2018b).

Differential coping This is when an individual may have different views on their treatment decisions from those of their family. Sedig (2016) notes that despite giving informed consent, a patient can struggle with the conflict between their desire to avoid further treatment and the additional psychological and emotional pain refusing treatment may cause for their family, who may wish them to undergo treatment in the hope of prolonging life.

Informed choice This allows patients and families make decisions that are consistent with their views, wishes, goals and values (Paterick et al, 2020).

THEORIES

Therapeutic relationship The relationship between the healthcare professional and patient involving the development of mutual trust and respect. This can be achieved by using effective verbal and non-verbal communication skills (Molina-Mula et al, 2020).

Identification of being in the last year of life *Earlier identification of people nearing the end of their life and inclusion on the register leads to earlier planning and better co-ordinated care* (Gold Standards Framework, 2011, p 1).

Active listening This requires that you listen, understand, respond to and reflect on what is being said, retaining the information which can enhance a trusting relationship (Delves-Yates, 2021b).

Loss and the grief response The loss may be physical (such as loss of function, loss of a limb, loss of a pet, the feeling of loss of control and loss of loved ones), social (such as divorce) or occupational (such as a job). Emotional reactions to grief can include anger, guilt, anxiety, sadness and despair (Oates and Maani-Fogelman, 2022).

Burnout This can commonly occur when you are in state of physical and emotional exhaustion and you experience long-term stress in your job, or when you have worked in a physically or emotionally draining role for a long time (NHS, 2022b).

Ethical principles Beauchamp and Childress's (2001) four medical ethics principles comprise one of the most widely used frameworks in healthcare. The principles are respect for autonomy, beneficence, non-maleficence and justice. The exploration of ethical issues that arise at the end of life is inherent to the work of palliative care. This is because the process of dying and death raises profound ethical questions about the meaning and value of human life.

Charter for Planning Ahead: What Matters Most (2020) Principles and questions to consider when planning for end-of-life decisions about treatment and care, useful for public and health and social care professionals alike.

Advance care planning This is used to enable people to express their future wishes and preferences about their treatment and different types of care and support when they reach the end of life (Cairns, 2011).

ReSPECT form (3rd edition) This stands for Recommended Summary Plan for Emergency Care and Treatment. It is a process which aims to develop a shared understanding between the healthcare professional and the patient in relation to their condition, the outcomes that the patient values and those they fear, and then how treatments and interventions, such as cardiopulmonary resuscitation, fit into this. It supports the important principle of personalised care (Resuscitation Council, 2020).

Advance directive Sometimes known as an advance decision to refuse treatment, an ADRT or a living will. This decision allows an individual to refuse a specific type of treatment at some time in the future (NHS, 2020).

Daffodil Standards These were created by the Royal College of General Practitioners (RCGP) and Marie Curie (2019). The standards are a blend of quality statements, evidence-based tools, reflective learning exercises and quality improvement activities for GP practices in the UK to support patients with an advanced serious illness or end-of-life care.

Total pain Dame Cicely Saunders, who pioneered the hospice movement, identified the model of 'total pain' which encompasses not only physical but psychological, social and spiritual pain.

APPROACHES

Symptom management This can include, for example, relief from pain, nausea and vomiting, restlessness or agitation and breathlessness. The provision of good symptom management in palliative and end-of-life care is associated with improved patient and family quality of life, greater treatment compliance, and may even offer survival advantages.

History taking This is a key component of patient assessment, allowing healthcare professionals to have a better understanding of patients' problems and enabling the delivery of high-quality care (Fawcett and Rhynas, 2012).

Pain assessment tools Tools that can be used to assess and measure the intensity of pain in an objective way. For further guidance see NICE (2021) on the assessment of pain.

Multidisciplinary team working Care whereby healthcare professionals work together to address the needs of the patient and promote excellent-quality care by exchanging their knowledge and skills (Taberna et al, 2020).

Informed consent In relation to treatment and care, informed consent means a person must have the understanding to give permission before they receive any type of medical treatment, test or examination or care. The person consenting must have the capacity to make the decision (NHS, 2019).

Continuity of care A person experiences an ongoing relationship with clinical teams in the delivery of services in a co-ordinated, coherent, logical and timely fashion (Ljungholm et al, 2022).

MODELS

SPIKES This is an example of one of the frameworks often used by healthcare professionals to guide them in breaking bad news. It can provide a helpful structure for communicating in a complex situation (Baile et al, 2000).

Calgary–Cambridge Communication Model (Silverman et al, 2013) This is a well-known approach to teaching communication skills. The model has five key steps to follow by enabling more accurate, efficient and supportive interviews, enhancing patient and professional experience and improving health outcomes for patients.

Reflection By using a reflective approach, health and care professionals can assess their experiences both positive and negative and explore where improvements to their practice may be needed (NMC, 2019).

Shared decision making This is a collaborative process in which patients and their healthcare providers make healthcare decisions together, considering the best scientific evidence, as well as the patient's values and preferences. The patient's role in making decisions will vary from person to person (Choosing Wisely, 2019; NICE Guidelines, 2019).

Analgesic ladder for cancer pain This was introduced in 1983 as a guide for health professionals in providing relief for cancer pain (Anekar and Cascella, 2022).

Further reading

General Medical Council (2022) Treatment and Care Towards the End of Life: Good Practice in Decision Making. [online] Available at: www.gmc-uk.org/ethical-guidance/ethical-guidance-for-doctors/treatment-and-care-towards-the-end-of-life (accessed 23 February 2023).

Mannix, K (2021) *Listen: How to Find the Words for Tender Conversations*. London: William Collins.

NHS (2020) Children and Bereavement. [online] Available at: www.nhs.uk/mental-health/children-and-young-adults/advice-for-parents/children-and-bereavement (accessed 23 February 2023).

NHS England (2022) *Ambitions for Palliative and End of Life Care: A National Framework for Local Action 2021–2026*. [online] Available at: www.england.nhs.uk/publication/ambitions-for-palliative-and-end-of-life-care-a-national-framework-for-local-action-2021-2026 (accessed 23 February 2023).

NHS England (2022) *Palliative and End of Life Care Statutory Guidance for Integrated Care Boards (ICBs)*. [online] Available at: www.england.nhs.uk/wp-content/uploads/2022/07/Palliative-and-End-of-Life-Care-Statutory-Guidance-for-Integrated-Care-Boards-ICBs-September-2022.pdf (accessed 23 February 2023).

Case study 14
Roger: a case of mistaken reality

Sarah Housden

Roger is 60 years old and has been diagnosed with young onset dementia. A sportsman by professional background, with a keen interest in football, he is currently being treated for widespread metastatic cancer, which has contributed to a rapid decline in his physical state of health, requiring admission to hospital over the weekend. Before meeting him, I have acquired some basic information on his health, background and dementia diagnosis.

MODEL: dementia syndrome

There had been some discussion about the suitability of the older person's medicine ward for someone of Roger's age, but the urgency of his admission and the rapidity of onset of breathing difficulties over the previous few days led to the conclusion that this was the best place for him for the time being, enabling tests to be carried out to determine the cause of his increased breathlessness.

My first meeting with Roger begins unexpectedly, soon after I arrive at work and have read through the handover sheet. As I walk from the reception area onto the ward, I am greeted by a warm and enthusiastic cheer from a lively looking grey-haired gentleman with a beaming smile, who appears to be waving to me from the nearest bay. I walk over to his bed and introduce myself by first name and my role within the ward. Roger laughs wheezily and gasps for breath in response. After some calming down, he points directly at me, his finger almost touching my chest and says: *'You're the best goal-keeper our team's ever had!'* The tone is simultaneously celebratory and accusatory, as if to correct my erroneous claim to be a member of hospital staff.

VALUE: 'Hello, my name is' campaign

I feel more than a little disconcerted by Roger's proclamation of my goal-keeping skills. I try to reason with myself – I'm in a uniform: perhaps this reminds him of a football kit in some way. It is possible that my long dark-blue trousers look like tracksuit bottoms in the evening light. He may have associated me with an actual person who plays football for the local team. I smile and nod, not wanting to disagree with Roger or undermine his good-humoured communication. As I walk away, smiling and nodding, I am unsure whether I have done the right thing. Roger's parting shot of: *'On the ball city!'* leaves me feeling some concern that by

APPROACH: sense-making

THEORIES: misidentification in dementia; well-being in dementia

VALUES: caring; honesty

not putting him right about who I am, I may have consolidated his perspective and taken him one step further away from reality.

Over the next few days, Roger maintains his understanding of me as a fellow sportsman, and as I spend more time with him, supporting him with personal care, it becomes clear that Roger thinks we are both working at what he believes to be a new elite sports facility in the city. Roger consistently recognises me as being a well-known and very successful goal-keeper and I keep the conversation going by asking him questions about his sporting career, without actually agreeing with his perspective on our current reality.

It is important to me to avoid doing Roger any harm, but I remain uncertain as to whether the best route to well-being for Roger, and to simultaneous integrity for me as a health practitioner, is via agreement or disagreement. I'm uncertain how to validate his identity and memories of lived experiences as a sportsman, at the same time as enabling him to orientate to the ward environment. Neither am I sure whether this is what is needed to provide the highest-quality patient-centred care to which I, and the hospital, aspire.

For the time being, I decide to maintain the status quo, by not arguing with him, but not correcting him either. 'After all', I say to my colleagues: 'Who is to say that any one of us has a monopoly on what reality is? We all think we're here as nurses and healthcare practitioners, but how can we be sure? We think we're right, but so does Roger and so do all the other patients with different perspectives on their current realities!' This seemed to be a good-humoured way of managing my unease and uncertainty about the extent to which providing good care involves collaborating with Roger's perspective or orientating him to mine.

'What do you think you're doing?' Another evening on the ward and the ward manager has noticed my interactions with Roger. Taking me to a side room, she reminds me of the need to orientate Roger to reality, as unpleasant as the reality is: that he is seriously unwell, meaning that he will never take part in any sporting event other than as a spectator again; that he is terminally ill and a patient in a hospital. However, the ward manager is clear in expressing her view that Roger needs to be supported in orientating to time and place; to go along with any other understanding of the situation amounts to collusion.

'Is there any wonder', she asks in a sharp tone, 'that these people get confused and disorientated on the ward? You have a professional responsibility to tell this gentleman the truth about his situation. How else can he adapt and participate properly in his care when he is being misled into thinking he is something and someone other than a patient?' The point she is making seems, on the surface, to be fair, and is one that I have turned over in my mind several times over the past few days.

At the same time, I know that Roger is so much more than a patient in a hospital bed. Within his mind, and through the re-living of his memories, with me as a trigger to support his vivid recall, he has had an opportunity to exist in what seems like a better place than his hospital bed. And whether or not he knows where he is, whether he has a cognitive impairment or not, he and every person with whom I work will always be more than the patient in front of me.

'Hello Roger, we need to get you ready to go for some X-rays.' I was back with Roger and trying to do as I had been advised. I certainly didn't want to do him any harm emotionally or otherwise, but I was still uncertain of the best way to orientate him to the reality of his current situation.

'Going for a training session then, are we?' he asks, eager-eyed. 'I don't know that I've got the energy – I haven't quite got my breath back after those last laps of the pitch.'

Swallowing my doubts, I try to orientate him gently, kindly: 'Oh Roger, right now there'll be no running around. I'm going to get someone with a wheelchair to take you. We need to get an X-ray done of your chest so that the doctor can get a better idea of what's going on in there.'

Roger looks at me, appearing more confused than I've seen him at any point until now. 'What are you talking about lad?' It feels like a betrayal of the trust I have built up with him, but I persevere: 'You're in hospital, Roger. You're quite unwell; do you remember what the doctor told you about the cancer?'

As if in fulfilment of all my fears of what orientating Roger to my reality would mean for him, I watch as he slowly withdraws into himself, lowering his head to rest his chin on his chest, as if surrendering to my reality. He isn't going to argue with me. There are no denials about this new perspective on the situation.

Though his sense of everyday reality is fragile, so is the reconstructed world of memories which helped to maintain his well-being and sense of himself as the well-known and admired sportsperson he has been for much of his adult life. Whatever was the harm in letting him experience that reality again? I am frustrated by my lack of skill in communicating his worth and validating his sense of self while simultaneously supporting him to navigate the harsh realities of his current situation. The dilemma saddens me. There seems to be no easy answer or straightforward approach that would enable me to juggle different perspectives on reality with people living with dementia.

Reflections

Person-centred practice is central to providing effective healthcare services to people of all ages and backgrounds, and across contexts of care. In the case of a person living with dementia, it is increasingly likely that support will be needed to maintain a sense of self and continuity of social identity in the context of experiences of increasing disability and dependence. At the same time, where short-term memory becomes less reliable, the person themself is likely to draw upon longer-term memory to express themself and retain their social self in interactions with those around them.

Memories of facts, and the ability to recall these, are processed largely by the hippocampus – an area of the brain affected early on in some types of dementia, such as Alzheimer's. As neuro-logical damage, and hence cognitive impairment, progresses, individuals living with dementia may still be able to retain a sense of how they feel within a relationship or during and after a specific interaction. This is due to emotional memories being processed largely within the amygdala, which remains relatively intact until the later stages of dementia. Had such ideas about the emotional impact of short-term memory loss been within the understanding of those involved in caring for Roger, it is likely that they would have worked towards finding some middle ground between their opposing perspectives on reality orientation.

There is never any doubt in this scenario that all staff want to enhance Roger's well-being. The difficulty lies in the different views on how best to do that, and the lack of drawing upon theory and evidence which relates specifically to best practice in delivering acute healthcare services for people living with dementia. On reflection, enhancing Roger's sense of self at the same time as enabling him to understand his current situation would be likely to involve combining reality orientation and reminiscence-based approaches to promoting well-being. Examples of this might be having laminated pictures of personal meaning to Roger at his bedside, with a brief orientating sign nearby stating the name of the hospital and ward, alongside an orientation clock stating the date as well as the time. These and other similar environmental features can implicitly prompt orientation so that Roger can more easily self-orientate. At the same time, personally meaningful pictures of sporting events are likely to encourage supportive conversations about his past which reinforce a sense of self.

These approaches take away the need to explicitly orientate Roger to a different perspective on reality, while validating his social and emotional self through discussions with ward staff on past sporting achievements – whether these be Roger's achievements or those of local teams, or even those of ward staff themselves. A combined approach to orientation and long-term memory stimulation has the potential to move Roger's care and all communications with him back into a person-centred framework, where his experiences and needs are central, and are catered for within the bounds of his abilities, in the context of progressive cognitive impairment.

Questions for reflection and discussion

1. To what extent do you agree or disagree with the statement made within this scenario, that going along with the reality of a person living with dementia who is reliving and orientated towards experiences from the past is a form of collusion?

2. Explain the potential benefits of combining approaches to enhancing well-being, such as validation, reality orientation and reminiscence, for people living with dementia and for their family and friends.

3. Explore and describe ways in which family members and friends of patients in a variety of contexts of care could be encouraged to support the use of meaningful pictures and objects while paying full attention to infection control guidelines and requirements.

4. In what ways could going along with patients' perspectives on reality without orientating them to their current situation compromise your integrity as a nurse?

5. How could avoiding arguing with the perspectives on reality held by patients living with dementia be seen as being aimed primarily at enhancing their well-being rather than as a potential threat to their well-being?

6. Is it ever right to withhold truth from a patient, or to lie to them, where this helps to keep them happy and maintain a peaceful environment?

Further information

VALUES

'Hello, my name is' campaign Dr Kate Granger, a medical doctor living with a terminal illness, began the 'Hello, my name is' campaign with her husband in 2013 to encourage and remind healthcare staff about the importance of introductions in healthcare. Further information is available on the campaign website: www.hellomynameis.org.uk

Caring Requires nurses to engage in interactions and interventions which focus on the needs of the whole person. Caring also includes making use of an evidence-based approach to providing the right care, in a timely way, at every stage of life.

Honesty This is an essential quality for any nurse due to the vulnerability of patients and service users who are unwell, and who may be dependent on the care and support of others. In dementia care, honesty and consistency are especially important in supporting a person to orientate themselves to reality and develop trust towards care and support staff who they may not consistently recognise.

Curiosity Involves going beyond the immediately obvious by observing, listening, asking questions and reflecting on the information gathered.

Professional integrity An essential quality of all nurses. Maintaining integrity in nursing practice has been described as requiring a continual balancing of *personal expectations, professional concerns and nursing realities* (Sastrawan et al, 2019, p 5).

Respect Involves recognising and acknowledging the value of all people living with dementia as individuals, in a way which enables them to maintain their dignity and self-respect.

Compassion Defined in *Compassion in Practice* as *how care is given through relationships based on empathy, respect and dignity* (Department of Health, 2012, p 13).

THEORIES

Misidentification in dementia A common experience where the person living with dementia mistakes someone for someone else, often someone from their past. The feelings they have towards the person in the present generally reflect those held towards the person from the past.

Well-being in dementia Described by Tom Kitwood (1997) as being attained when a person's needs for love, occupation, comfort, identity, attachment and inclusion are met. Signs of well-being include having a sense of identity, being connected with others, feeling secure, being able to act autonomously, finding meaning, growth as a person and individual, and enjoyment of life.

Therapeutic lying Also known as benevolent or prosocial lying and involves telling lies that *are told in the best interests of a person with dementia, to avoid distress or harm that may be derived from an act of truth-telling* (Wheaton, 2022, p 2241). The acceptability of lying to a person living with dementia is a hotly debated topic, especially in view of the fluctuating nature of cognitive ability, including memory, in some types of dementia.

Cognitive impairment This can be defined as difficulty with processing thoughts which can lead to changes in memory, decision-making skills, concentration and attention, and difficulty learning new information.

Disorientation of time and place A state of mental confusion arising in dementia due to neurological changes which have led to cognitive impairments. Specific aspects of disorientation in dementia can include loss of a sense of time, self-hood, direction and place.

Different perspectives on reality The recognition that everyone has a unique perspective on reality. This can lead to complex disagreements about reality in dementia care, where an individual living with dementia may have perceptual difficulties in addition to disorientation of time and place.

Non-maleficence The principle within ethical healthcare practice to 'do no harm'.

Inner conflict Involves an internal battle, which can lead to a sense of cognitive dissonance.

Acceptance of loss The grief experience has been described as involving five stages of processing a loss, one of which is acceptance (Kubler-Ross and Kessler, 2014).

Identity Within social psychology, identity is understood to be both individual and to be grounded in a social context. Where identity is threatened, individuals are likely to hold more firmly to a role they have held, or to a sense of belonging to a group which they previously experienced as being important to them.

Nurses acting as advocates Involves ensuring that every patient is heard and understood.

APPROACHES

Sense-making The process through which people make sense of their experiences. It can be done simultaneously with the experience or retrospectively, individually or as a group.

Communication This is *'central to successful caring relationships and to effective team working. Listening is as important as what we say and do'* (Department of Health, 2012, p 13).

Validation Recognises the importance of validating the emotional aspects and expressed feelings within the experiences of people living with dementia. Feelings can be validated by asking about how a person feels about a place or time of life, without agreeing or disagreeing that this is factually the case now.

Life history and life story Draw upon the experiences of people living with dementia from across their lifespan, rather than just seeing the person as they are in the here and now.

Reality orientation Supports the orientation of a person living with dementia, using environmental cues and conversational prompts, as well as information boards, clocks, calendars and signage, all of which are aimed at helping the person remember where they are and to remain orientated to the present.

Conflict avoidance Using this a strategy within nursing potentially only delays facing a difficult situation. While it can be seen as potentially removing heated arguments out of the public eye as a way of resolving disputes professionally, there is also a significant risk of avoiding opportunities to resolve the conflict.

Reflective practice The NMC require reflections as part of the revalidation process. Many teams conduct monthly reflective practice groups as a useful approach to improving practice.

MODELS

Dementia syndrome The term 'dementia' refers to a wide-ranging group of brain diseases, all of which lead to progressive cognitive impairment. The type (or types) of dementia affecting any individual is determined by where in the brain the disease process begins, and by the mechanism of disease which is destroying brain cells. Over 200 types of neurological impairment have been identified as belonging under the umbrella of the family of dementias. Young onset dementia is defined as any dementia where the onset of symptoms occurs before age 65. Dementia has been identified as a 'syndrome' because the lived experience of dementia is determined not only by the neurological damage, but also by internal and external factors influencing the person's social, emotional and physical environment. For further information on this understanding of dementias, see the work of Tom Kitwood (1997).

Memory Can be understood in terms of models which enable understanding of how it works. For example, the two types of memory (explicit memory and implicit memory) and the three major memory stages (sensory, short-term and long-term) were originally outlined by Atkinson and Shiffrin (1968). In addition, the three processes of encoding, storage and retrieval provide an understanding of how we lay down, maintain and recall long-term memories.

Person-centred care Depends on a therapeutic relationship between the nurse and patient that is built on effective communication, and has patients' needs, values and choices central to the development of care delivery (Gluyas, 2015).

Further reading

Brooker, D and Latham, I (2016) *Person-Centred Dementia Care: Making Services Better with the VIPS Framework*. 2nd ed. London: Jessica Kingsley Publishers.

Culley, H, Barber, R, Hope, A and James, I (2013) Therapeutic Lying in Dementia Care. *Nursing Standard*, 28(1): 35–9.

Feil, N and de Klerk-Rubin, V (2012) *The Validation Breakthrough: Simple Techniques for Communicating with People with Alzheimer's and Other Dementias*. 3rd ed. Baltimore, MD; London; Sydney: Health Professions Press.

Hayo, H, Ward, A and Parkes, J (2018) *Young Onset Dementia: A Guide to Recognition, Diagnosis, and Supporting Individuals with Dementia and their Families*. London: Jessica Kingsley Publishers.

James, J, Cotton, B, Knight, J, Freyne, R, Pettit, J and Gilby, L (2017) *Excellent Dementia Care in Hospitals: A Guide to Supporting People with Dementia and their Carers*. London: Jessica Kingsley Publishers.

Case study 15
Lucy: the man I plan to marry

Katrina Emerson

Friday afternoon's walk-in contraceptive and sexual health clinic is the one I least enjoy. The clinic is always busy and, because there are no bookable appointments, the wait time can be long and tempers often become frayed. Cathy, my favourite receptionist, brings me a very welcome cup of coffee and a piece of cake (the only good thing about Friday is that it is cake day!) and I browse the appointments to check who I am seeing next. Looking at the list, I can see this is Lucy, a new patient who has never attended the service before. As this is Lucy's first time with us, I quickly finish my coffee and cake and hurry to the waiting room. For a new patient, sitting in a busy waiting room can be quite daunting, particularly if they are attending the clinic on their own.

The waiting area is heaving with people, and I quickly scan the room to see if I can spot someone who could be Lucy. There is a young woman sitting by the window anxiously picking the skin around her nails and looking as if she might bolt for the door at any moment; I take a gamble and say her name, '*Lucy?*' She nods hesitantly and I ask if she would like to come with me. We walk in silence to the consulting room and when inside, I ask her to take a seat.

As Lucy settles herself, takes off her coat and puts away her mobile phone, I take the opportunity to observe her verbal and non-verbal body language. Lucy appears to be very anxious; she avoids eye contact and constantly pulls the sleeves of her cardigan over her hands. This behaviour does not concern me unduly; Lucy's anxiety is a common response for someone attending the clinic for the first time and something I take into consideration. I suspect Lucy has a range of anxieties and concerns and it is important that I use the first few minutes of the consultation to put her at her ease.

VALUE: communication

VALUE: empathy and compassion

VALUE: empathy and compassion

The British Association for Sexual Health and HIV (BASHH) guidelines (BASHH, 2019) highlight key factors essential when taking a sexual history. Central to the BASHH guidance is the need for the discussion to be confidential, the environment welcoming and the practitioner non-judgemental, knowledgeable and experienced with effective communication skills. I am using the Calgary–Cambridge model (Silverman et al, 2013) to structure the consultation.

I start by introducing myself and my role and invite Lucy to call me Katrina. I also check if Lucy's happy for me to call her by her first name. From experience I know how important the first few minutes of the consultation will be for establishing trust with Lucy. I am also mindful that the way in which I manage Lucy's first appointment will determine whether she returns for follow-up. I establish I have the right '*Lucy*' by checking her date of birth corresponds with the details on the electronic records. Lucy confirms her date of birth and I note she has just had her sixteenth birthday. At this point, I deliberately turn to face the computer screen; this allows Lucy to familiarise herself with her surroundings and to appraise me. From experience, I know these strategies help us develop a rapport. As I check Lucy's details, I comment on the vibrant red of her nail polish and she invites me to look at her thumbs, which have tiny stars embedded in the varnish. I show her my '*nurse's hands*' and bemoan the fact that I cannot have painted nails. I sense Lucy is beginning to relax with me, which is my intention.

Lucy and I continue to chat for a while longer; she tells me she has just started a course in travel and tourism at the local sixth form college and we talk about college and how she is finding the course. I nod and smile to show I am listening, and I decide not to mention I regularly work in the sexual health outreach clinic held in the college health centre as Lucy may become fearful that I might share information about her with her tutors or speak to her when she is with her peers.

When I feel Lucy has relaxed enough to engage with the session, I begin the consultation. I am mindful that one of the main barriers for young people accessing contraceptive and sexual health advice are their concerns around confidentiality, so I start by asking Lucy what she understands about the service and in particular the level of confidentiality she can expect. Lucy tells me her boyfriend said we are the best people to see as we are not allowed to tell anyone she has attended. Lucy is particularly keen her parents are not informed, stating they do not know about Ben and would not approve of him. I explain that while, in most cases, we will not share her information, under certain circumstances it may be necessary for me to make a referral to another professional. I go on to say that should this be needed, I would discuss this with her before doing so.

APPROACH: sexual history

People attending sexual health services do so in the knowledge they will receive a free, non-judgemental and confidential service and that no information will be shared without their knowledge and consent. However, if during the consultation it becomes apparent there are concerns regarding Lucy's welfare or safety, an appropriate referral will be made. It is important practitioners are explicit regarding the level of confidentiality an individual can expect and the circumstances in which it might be breached (Faculty of Sexual and Reproductive Healthcare (FSRH) Guidelines, 2016).

Lucy seems happy with this, and we continue with the appointment. I ask Lucy why she is attending today, and she nervously tells me she would like contraceptive advice. She explains that she and her partner, Ben, have been together for a couple of months and have recently started a sexual relationship. To date, they have been using condoms, but Ben does not like them and on a couple of occasions has refused to use one. I check when Lucy's last menstrual period was to establish pregnancy risk; I am reassured when she says she is currently menstruating. Lucy proudly tells me Ben has been researching suitable contraception on the internet and he thinks the implant would be a good option. I am aware, in some circumstances, that seeing couples together can be an effective means of increasing contraceptive use. I ask whether Ben has accompanied Lucy today and, if so, would she like him to join us? Lucy shakes her head and says he is far too busy to attend and anyway 'it wouldn't be a good idea'. I decide to pick this up at a later stage in the consultation.

THEORY: contraceptive consultation

THEORY: contraceptive consultation

VALUE: communication

Lucy and I chat about her relationship. Ben is her first 'proper' boyfriend, and she is keen to tell me how generous and kind he is, always buying her expensive gifts. She waggles her arm in front of me to show me a lovely silver charm bracelet, her most recent present. Lucy also shows me a small diamond engagement ring which she wears on a chain around her neck. Ben, she tells me conspiratorially, is keen to marry as soon as Lucy finishes college. Lucy goes on to say that she hides the presents from her parents as she knows they will not be happy. I ask Lucy if Ben has a job. She looks nervously around the room and says yes but does not elaborate further.

APPROACH: safeguarding

Ordinarily, as Lucy is 16 years old, there is no requirement for me to follow the Fraser Guidelines for assessing her competency for contraceptive and sexual health advice. Had Lucy been younger, I would have been required to document that I had followed the under-16 guidance to establish Lucy's competency to make informed decisions regarding her care. However, Lucy's comments about Ben advising her to attend the clinic, his involvement with the choice of contraception and his ability to buy expensive gifts for Lucy make me feel a little uncomfortable. This may well mean nothing, but I feel I need to explore further. I ask Lucy how she met Ben; Lucy explains they had met on her first day at the college in the canteen; he was the second person to speak to her. This provides me with some reassurance; if Ben is attending the same college, they must be roughly the same age, suggesting my fears are unfounded. In young people over the age of 16 years, the FSRH 2016 Guidelines advise practitioners to establish that there are no exploitation or safeguarding issues and that consent to sexual activity is voluntary and without coercion.

VALUE: non-judgemental care

MODEL: Fraser Guidelines

VALUE: choice

As part of a contraceptive consultation, it is helpful for me to establish why the current method is unacceptable; this will help Lucy make an informed choice when thinking about options going forward. As such, I am keen to understand why Ben dislikes condoms and establish whether there are practical issues such as allergy or fit. While most contraceptive methods are an effective means of preventing pregnancy, the majority do not protect against sexually transmitted infections such as chlamydia. When providing sexual health advice, it is important to raise awareness of the need to practise safer sex as well as preventing unplanned pregnancies and where possible to continue with condom use.

THEORY: contraceptive consultation

In addition to providing contraceptive advice, an important aspect of the sexual health consultation is providing general sexual health advice to raise awareness of sexually transmitted diseases (STIs) and their modes of transmission. With younger people this advice should include where to obtain free condoms, correct use, how to access STI screening and the availability and provision of emergency contraception (EC) (FSRH Guidelines, 2016).

Lucy looks a little embarrassed and mumbles something about Ben finding condoms uncomfortable and messy. I explain this is a common problem due to poor technique and I would be happy to see Ben in clinic to talk through condom application and, if

Ben and Lucy would like, they could attend together. Lucy giggles and mutters something about Ben being unlikely to need my advice. She then appears to change the subject, asking whether her mum would be able to see an implant should she decide to have one. We continue to talk in general about the various contraceptive options available for Lucy and the relative pros and cons in terms of acceptability and levels of involvement. I am particular that Lucy being 16 years old should not limit her choice and we explore the various forms of contraception including intrauterine methods. I explain to Lucy that whichever method she chooses will need to be acceptable to her and compatible with her lifestyle. For example, injectables might not be appropriate if Lucy has a fear of needles. Similarly, while a highly effective method of contraception, Lucy might find inserting a vaginal ring into the vagina unacceptable. I explain that while an implant would be ideal in some ways, she will have to wear a dressing on her arm for a few days post-insertion and she needs to think about what she might tell her parents. Lucy states she absolutely cannot have a dressing and asks what else she might use. I reassure Lucy that there are a range of contraceptive options available to her; we just need to check she does not have any underlying health conditions which might mean some types of contraception are unsuitable. For example, there is a link between the combined oral contraceptive pill and increased risk of stroke in women with a history of migraine with an aura.

VALUE: non-judgemental care

VALUE: choice

VALUE: choice

THEORY: contraceptive consultation

As a reproductive and sexual health practitioner, I use the United Kingdom Medical Eligibility Criteria for Contraceptive Use (UKMEC) (FSRH, 2016) as a decision-making tool when helping people select their preferred method of contraception. The UKMEC Guidelines are based on contemporary research and evidence and are a robust and effective decision-making tool for practitioners ensuring both efficacy and safety of method.

I am impressed by Lucy's knowledge of her own health and that of her immediate family; it is unusual for someone to be so well-prepared. She has clearly done her research and knows what we will need to establish for me to prescribe the most appropriate contraceptive for her needs. Lucy suffers from headaches; these, we establish, are not migraine with aura as she does not experience vision loss, sensory changes or muscle weakness. They tend to be associated with stress and tiredness and are easily resolved with over-the-counter analgesia. Both her parents are fit and healthy and, to her knowledge, neither have been prescribed any form of regular medication. Lucy's periods are regular (every 28 days), and her body mass index and blood pressure are within normal ranges. I reassure her that she is 'perfect', and she laughs. Ben had told her I would need to take a medical history to check suitability of method; again, this seems a little odd to me, but I let it go.

APPROACH: sexual history

Lucy and I discuss the range of contraceptives available to her (12 plus) and we talk about acceptability and suitability of the methods and level of commitment required by Lucy. She is not keen on injectables, viewing the regular appointments and frequent injections as an inconvenience. Despite reassurance, the idea of a wound dressing has put her off the implant and she is worried her mum might notice a contraceptive patch. She is quite interested in the vaginal ring, so I begin to talk through the literature with her and show her the demonstration 'ring'. Lucy asks if the ring is like the contraceptive diaphragm as she has read this needs to be inserted a few hours before intercourse; this she states would not be suitable for her. I reassure her this is not the case, but I am interested in why this might be a problem. If Lucy is reluctant to insert a diaphragm into her vagina, the vaginal ring would not be an acceptable method either. Lucy is quick to reassure me this is not the issue as she and Ben mainly have sex in his car.

VALUE: choice

This rings alarm bells with me; while it is not unusual for a 17 year-old to hold a driver's license and have access to or own a car, it seems odd this is Ben and Lucy's preferred place for intimacy. I ask Lucy whether they ever have sex anywhere other than the car and she replies: 'We did it at college a couple of times, but it felt too risky' and 'we booked a hotel but the lady on reception wasn't very nice to Ben'. Lucy has already told me her parents do not know about Ben and would not approve; I ask her whether she has been to Ben's home or met his family yet.

Lucy looks anxiously around the room, and I wonder, for a split second, whether she might bolt for the door. Something I have said has clearly upset her and when she turns to face me, I can see she is both frightened but also very angry. 'Why', she asks defensively, 'cannot you just get on with your job and stop asking questions which are none of your business? Why does it matter to you where Ben and me meet or if I have met his family; none of this has anything to do with you or anyone else?' I know I will need to give Lucy time to calm down before we proceed with the consultation. Eventually, when Lucy's anger has subsided and her body language suggests she is a little more settled, I ask whether there is a reason she is worried about people knowing about her and Ben's relationship. *'If people find out'*, she says, *'Ben will get into trouble, and it will be all my fault.'* I ask Lucy why.

Lucy scrabbles in her handbag and pulls out a paper tissue; she is becoming increasingly tearful. Ben, it turns out, is married with a baby. Lucy is confident his marriage is an unhappy one as Ben has told her so. Lucy states that Ben is planning to leave his wife just as soon as his small son starts school. She begs me not to tell anyone as Ben might get into trouble. I am becoming increasingly concerned for Lucy's welfare and I ask why she thinks Ben may get into trouble, explaining that while he is older and married, there is nothing to stop him seeing Lucy. Lucy sobs loudly, *'if the college find out, Ben will lose his job'*. I ask Lucy what it is Ben does. Ben, it turns out, is Lucy's tutor. I take Lucy's hand and tell her that I need to consult the clinic's safeguarding lead. I explain that Ben is in a position of responsibility and is not allowed professionally to have relationships with his students. It is my duty to protect her from being exploited. Lucy is crying now and saying I had promised her I would not tell anyone, and she wishes now that she had never spoken to me or attended the clinic. I tell her that I will go and discuss her case with my colleague so that Lucy can be assured that I am acting correctly and in her best interests.

APPROACH: *safeguarding*

While the legal age for consent to sexual activity is 16 years, this is not the case where a person is in a position of responsibility and working with children (defined as under 18 years). In this instance, a referral must be made to the Local Authority Designated Officer (LADO), the individual responsible for co-ordinating allegations made against any adult who works with children.

Reflections

Reflecting on the consultation, I realise I missed several opportunities to establish Ben's age and relationship with Lucy. Despite concerns regarding the balance of power within the relationship I was happy to be reassured by Lucy that Ben was of a similar age to her and that there were no safeguarding issues. I had focused too much on reassuring Lucy and putting her at ease and in so doing I had offered her false reassurance. Lucy mentioning gifts, the apparent need for secrecy and her reluctance for Ben to attend the appointment were all safeguarding red flags that I should have explored further. Furthermore, while I am confident I gave clear messages regarding confidentiality, I could have checked Lucy fully understood there might be some circumstances where this was beyond my gift. I needed to listen more to what Lucy was not saying rather than to what she said.

Questions for reflection and discussion

1. How might Lucy have reacted had I asked how old Ben was at the start of the consultation?

2. Why in this scenario is sex not deemed consensual?

3. Lucy does not consider herself vulnerable and this will make it difficult to understand the need for the intervention. How could one justify this to Lucy?

4. How could one support Lucy from this point onwards?

5. Are there any other circumstances where a nurse might need to breach confidentiality?

6. How should you assess capacity in a sexual health consultation and does the Mental Capacity Act 2005 apply in this scenario?

Further information

VALUES

Communication In sexual health, communication includes using appropriate language and terminology to avoid misunderstanding, confusion or embarrassment.

Empathy and compassion Sexual health practitioners must be non-judgemental and be careful to avoid embarrassment by using appropriate language and terminology.

Confidentiality When working with young people requesting sexual health advice, it is important to be clear regarding the circumstances in which confidentiality can and cannot be guaranteed.

Non-judgemental care Involves healthcare workers seeking permission, avoiding assumptions and demonstrating empathy, genuineness and acceptance of individuals in their care.

Choice Together with acceptability of contraceptive methods, choice can help with adherence. Choice of method might be influenced by the myths and misconceptions of external influences such as friends and family.

THEORIES

Consultation skills A framework used to structure patient/nurse interaction.

Contraceptive consultation A means of establishing individual preference, level of involvement, safety and the successes or failures of previous contraceptive methods.

APPROACHES

Sexual history A means of assessing and screening individuals who have concerns regarding their sexual health.

Safeguarding In every consultation the practitioner needs to assess whether a relationship is consensual and not abusive or coercive.

MODELS

Fraser Guidelines A tool to help practitioners decide whether they should and are able to prescribe contraception to young people between the ages of 13 and 16 years without parental consent. The guidelines apply specifically to providing advice and treatment to under 16s accessing contraception and sexual health advice.

Further reading

Delves-Yates, C (2021) *Beginner's Guide to Reflective Practice in Nursing*. London: Sage Publications.

Everett, S (2021) *Handbook of Contraception and Sexual Health*. 4th ed. London: Routledge.

Ingham, R and Aggleton, P (2006) *Promoting Young People's Sexual Health: International Perspectives*. London: Routledge.

Melville, C (2015) *Sexual and Reproductive Health at a Glance*. Chichester: Wiley-Blackwell.

Ryan-Morgan, T (2021) *A Concise Guide to the Mental Capacity Act: Basic Principles in Practice*. London: Routledge.

Conclusion

Julia Hubbard

I hope you found the case studies in this book interesting and that they stimulated you to undertake further reading and supported you to reflect on your own decision-making skills in practice. The range and types of decisions and dilemmas nurses encounter every day are exemplified by these case studies, which clearly demonstrate the importance of reflection both in and on action and using the highest-quality available contemporary evidence with which to support decisions. The case studies have hopefully encouraged you to think beyond the narrow biomedical/clinical determinants of decision making and to consider service users' psychosocial, spiritual and politico-economic worldviews.

You may have identified several reoccurring themes across the case studies, for example, safeguarding (children and adults), person-centred care, consent, assessment, communication and ethical principles which explicitly demonstrate the application of the '6 Cs' – care, compassion, competence, communication, courage and commitment (NHS England, 2017). The case studies also show how nurses' values and behaviour should be guided by the Code (NMC, 2018b), reminding us of the expected professional conduct of nurses, midwives and nursing associates in the UK.

Moving forward with your own clinical practice and the dilemmas and decision making you will encounter, I have provided a few decision-making pitfalls to be aware of in Table C.1.

Anchoring bias	being overly reliant on the first piece of information
Clustering illusion	tendency to see patterns in random events
Blind spot bias	not noticing either cognitive or motivational bias in ourselves
Ostrich effect	ignoring dangerous or negative information
Resource bias	decisions actively influenced by availability of resources
Availability heuristic	overestimating the importance of available information
Confirmation bias	listening only to information which confirms our pre-conceptions
Recency bias	weighting latest information more heavily than previous evidence
Over-optimism	too confident in our decision and taking greater risks
Repetition bias	tendency to attach weight to the most repeated story
Similarity bias	favouring the information presented by people who are 'like us'
Conservatism bias	favouring prior evidence over up-to-date information
Group think bias	safety in numbers makes people reluctant to appear to think differently from the group
Sunk-costs bias	following through on a course of action because we previously invested in it
Authority bias	basing decisions on the attributes and opinions of an authority figure and putting personal opinion on hold

Table C.1 Decision pitfalls

(Jackson, 2021)

Interestingly, the more experienced and confident we become, the more biased we tend to become (Jackson, 2021). For instance, if we have encountered something similar previously, we are more likely to draw comparisons the next time. Although this means that exposure to nursing practice brings valuable clinical judgement, it may also mean we take shortcuts with our decision making (Jackson, 2021). As mentioned in the introduction, we bring our own worldview and sometimes the influences of our home lives to situations, which at times can cloud our judgement. Always use the team around you when feasible to guard against any unconscious bias (Oxtoby, 2020).

In conclusion, working in a caring role can be profoundly rewarding as being alongside others when they are at their most vulnerable and scared is both a privilege and incredibly fulfilling. When you began your career in nursing, you may have had high expectations of yourself and given little thought to the impact of this type of work on your daily life either physically or emotionally. However, nursing in the real world can be difficult at times and the most important thing to remember is to give yourself permission to look after yourself and have some self-compassion. Take time to support and reassure your work colleagues and do not hesitate to reach out for support when you need it. Keep alert to the signs of compassion fatigue, stress or burnout and take proactive steps to avoid these in the first place. See the further reading for sources of advice and support of where to get help. Finally, remember that if you feel well both physically and mentally you can provide the highest-quality and most compassionate experience for those in your care.

Further reading

Cavell Nurses Trust (2022) Help and Advice. [online] Available at: https://cavellnursestrust.org (accessed 19 December 2022).

NHS England (2021) Professional Nurse Advocate Programme. [online] Available at: www.england.nhs.uk/nursingmidwifery/delivering-the-nhs-ltp/professional-nurse-advocate (accessed 5 January 2023).

Nurse Lifeline (nd) Supporting Mental Health and Emotional Wellbeing. [online] Available at: www.nurselifeline.org.uk (accessed 4 January 2023).

Nursing and Midwifery Council (NMC) (2020) Mental Health and Wellbeing. [online] Available at: https://nmc.org.uk/news/news-and-updates/mental-health-wellbeing/ (accessed 19 December 2022).

Royal College of Nursing (2015). Stress and You: A Guide for Nursing Staff. [online] Available at: www.rcn.org.uk/professinal-development/publications/pub-004967 (accessed 20 December 2022).

Royal College of Nursing (2019) Beating Burn Out. [online] Available at: www.rcn.org.uk/magazines/bulletin/2019/november/beating-burnout (accessed 5 January 2023).

Royal College of Nursing Counselling Service (nd) [online] Available at: www.rcn.org.uk/Get-Help/Member-support-services (accessed 23 February 2023).

References

Akyirem, S, Salifu, Y, Bayuo, J, Duodu, P A, Bossman, I F and Abboah-Offei, M (2022) An Integrative Review of the Use of the Concept of Reassurance in Clinical Practice. *Nursing Open*, 9(3): 1515–35.

Alladin, W (1998) Models of Counselling and Psychotherapy for a Multiethnic Society. In Palmer, S and Laungani, P (eds) *Counselling in a Multicultural Society* (pp 90–112). Oxford: Sage.

Ali, M (2018) Communication Skills 5: Effective Listening and Observation. *Nursing Times*, 114(4): 56–7.

Andover, M S and Morris, B W (2014) Expanding and Clarifying the Role of Emotion Regulation in Non-suicidal Self-injury. *Canadian Journal of Psychiatry. Revue canadienne de psychiatrie*, 59(11): 569–75.

Anekar, A and Cascella, M (2022) WHO Analgesic Ladder. StatPearls Publishing. [online] Available at: www.ncbi.nlm.nih.gov/books/NBK554435 (accessed 23 February 2023).

Asmussen, K, Fischer, F, Drayton, E and McBride, T (2020) Adverse Childhood Experiences: What We Know, What We Don't Know, and What Should Happen Next. Early Intervention Foundation. [online] Available at: www.eif.org.uk/report/adverse-childhood-experiences-what-we-know-what-we-dont-know-and-what-should-happen-next (accessed 23 February 2023).

Atkinson, R C and Shiffrin, R M (1968) Human Memory: A Proposed System and its Control Processes. In Spence, K (ed) *The Psychology of Learning and Motivation* (vol 2, pp 89–195). Oxford: Academic Press.

Baile, W, Buckman, R, Lenzi, R, Glober, G, Beale, E and Kudelka, A (2000) SPIKES: A Six-Step Protocol for Delivering Bad News: Application to the Patient with Cancer. *Oncologist*, 5(4): 302–11.

Bandura, A (1977) *Social Learning Theory*. 2nd ed. Hoboken, NJ: Prentice Hall.

Bateman, A, Brown, D and Peddar, J (2010) *Introduction to Psychotherapy: An Outline of Psychodynamic Principles and Practice*. 4th ed. Abingdon: Routledge.

Beauchamp, T and Childress, J (2001) *Principles of Biomedical Ethics*. 5th ed. Oxford: Oxford University Press.

Bogle, A and Go, S (2015) Breaking Bad (News) Death-Telling in the Emergency Department. *Journal of Missouri Medicine*, 112(1): 12–16.

Boullier, M and Blair, M (2018) Adverse Childhood Experiences. *Paediatrics and Child Health*, 28(3): 132–7.

Bowlby, J (1968) *Attachment and Loss. Vol 1: Attachment*. New York: Basic Books.

British Association for Sexual Health and HIV (BASHH) (2019) *United Kingdom National Guideline for Consultations Requiring Sexual History Taking*. Clinical Effectiveness Group, British Association for Sexual Health, and HIV. [online] Available at: www.bashhguidelines.org/media/1239/2019-sexual-history-guidelines-final.pdf (accessed 23 February 2023).

British Liver Trust (2022) Hepatitis C. [online] Available at: https://britishlivertrust.org.uk/information-and-support/living-with-a-liver-condition/liver-conditions/hepatitis-c-2 (accessed 23 February 2023).

Brown, A, Hayden, S, Klingman, K and Hussey, L (2020) Managing Uncertainty in Chronic Illness from Patient Perspectives. *Journal of Excellence in Nursing and Healthcare Practice*, 2(2): 1–6.

Bury, M (1982) Chronic Illness as Biographical Disruption. *Sociology of Health and Illness*, 4(2): 167–82.

Cairns, R (2011) Advance Care Planning: Thinking Ahead to Achieve Our Patients' Goals. *British Journal of Community Nursing*, 16(9): 427.

Care and Support Statutory Guidance (2022) [online] Available at: www.gov.uk/government/publications/care-act-statutory-guidance/care-and-support-statutory-guidance (accessed 23 February 2023).

Care Quality Commission (2015) *Statement on CQC's Roles and Responsibilities for Safeguarding Children and Adults*. [online] Available at: www.cqc.org.uk/sites/default/files/20150710_CQC_New_Safeguarding_Statement.pdf (accessed 9 December 2022).

Carper, B A (1978) Fundamental Patterns of Knowing in Nursing. *Advances in Nursing Science*, 1: 13–24.

Center for Disease Control and Prevention (2020) *'Revolving Door' Syndrome*. [online] Available at: wwwn.cdc.gov/WPVHC/Nurses/Course/Slide/Unit3_11 (accessed 23 February 2023).

Chapman, H (2017) Nursing Theories 1: Person-Centred Care. *Nursing Times*, 113(10): 59.

Charmaz, K (1991) *Good Days, Bad Days: The Self in Chronic Illness and Time*. New Brunswick, NJ: Rutgers University Press.

Charter for Planning Ahead: What Matters Most (2020) [online] Available at: www.whatmattersconversations.org/2020-charter (accessed 23 February 2023).

Child Safeguarding Practice Review Panel (2022) *Bruising in Non-Mobile Infants: Panel Briefing*. London: HM Government.

Children Act (1989) *Working Together to Safeguard Children: Statutory Framework*. [online] Available at: https://assets.publishing.service.gov.uk (accessed 12 December 2022).

Choosing Wisely UK (2019) *Shared Decision Making*. [online] Available at: www.choosingwisely.co.uk/shared-decision-making-resources (accessed 23 February 2023).

Christian, M S, Bradley, J C, Wallace, J C and Burke, M (2009) Workplace Safety: A Meta-analysis of the Roles of Person and Situation Factors. *Journal of Applied Psychology*, 94(5): 1103–27.

Cobb, J, Girauld, A and Kerr, M (2008) Health Checks and People with Learning Disability. *Tizard Learning Disability Review*. [online] Available at: www-emerald-com.uea.idm.oclc.org/insight/cont ent/doi/10.1108/13595474200800028/full/pdf?title=health-checks-and-people with-learning-disabilities (accessed 10 January 2023).

Compas, B E, Jaser, S S, Dunbar, J P, Watson, K H, Bettis, A H, Gruhn, M A and Williams, E K (2014) Coping and Emotion Regulation from Childhood to Early Adulthood: Points of Convergence and Divergence. *Australian Journal of Psychology*, 66(2): 71–81.

Cooper, S and Wakelam, A (1999) Leadership of Resuscitation Teams: 'Lighthouse Leadership'. *Resuscitation*, 42(1): 27–45.

Copperman, J and Brown, H (2021) Managing Safeguarding Across Health and Social Care. In MacKian, S and Simons, J (eds) *Leading, Managing, Caring* (pp 377–400). Abingdon: Routledge.

Coy, M and Kelly, L (2011) *Islands in the Stream: An Evaluation of Four London Independent Domestic Violence Advocacy Schemes.* London: Trust for London.

Cutlip, S and Center, A (2005) *Effective Public Relations*. 9th ed. London: Prentice Hall.

Daffodil Standards (2019) [online] Available at: www.mariecurie.org.uk/professionals/working-in-partnership/royal-college-of-gps/daffodil-standards (accessed 23 February 2023).

Dall'Ora, C and Saville, C (2021) Burnout in Nursing: What Have We Learnt and What Is Still Unknown? *Nursing Times*, 117(2): 43–4.

Delves-Yates, C (2021a) *Beginner's Guide to Reflective Practice in Nursing*. London: Sage Publications.

Delves-Yates, C (2021b) *Essentials of Nursing Practice*. London: Sage.

Department for Education (2018a) *Information Sharing: Advice for Practitioners Providing Safeguarding Services to Children, Young People, Parents, and Carers*. London: HM Government.

Department for Education (2018b) *Working Together to Safeguard Children: A Guide to Inter-agency Working to Safeguard and Promote the Welfare of Children*. London: HM Government.

Department of Health (2011) *Guidance and Toolkit for Vulnerable Adult Interventions*. London: HM Government.

Department of Health (2012) *Compassion in Practice: Nursing, Midwifery and Care Staff; Our Vision and Strategy*. Gateway reference 18479. London: HM Government.

Department of Health & Social Care (2021) NHS Constitution for England. London: HM Government. [online] Available at: www.gov.uk/government/publications/the-nhs-constitution-for-england/the-nhs-constitution-for-england (accessed 12 December 2022).

Dithole, K S, Thupayagale-Tshweneagae, G, Akpor, A O and Moleki, M M (2017) Communication Skills Intervention: Promoting Effective Communication Between Nurses and Mechanically Ventilated Patients. *Biomedical Centre Nurse*, 16(74): 1–6.

Duluth Model (2022) [online] Available at: www.theduluthmodel.org/wheels (accessed 12 December 2022).

Dunkley, C (2020) *Regulating Emotion the DBT Way: A Therapist's Guide to Opposite Action*. London: Routledge.

Early Intervention Foundation (2020) *Adverse Childhood Experiences: What We Know, What We Don't Know, and What Should Happen Next*. [online] Available at: www.eif.org.uk/report/adverse-childhood-experiences-what-we-know-what-we-dont-know-and-what-should-happen-next (accessed 23 February 2023).

Faculty of Sexual and Reproductive Healthcare (FSRH) (2016, amended 2019) *UK Medical Eligibility Criteria for Contraceptive Use (UKMEC)*. [online] Available at: www.fsrh.org/documents/ukmec-2016 (accessed 23 February 2023).

Farre, A and Rapley, T (2017) The New Old (and Old New) Medical Model: Four Decades Navigating the Biomedical and Psychosocial Understandings of Health and Illness. *Healthcare*, 5(4): 88.

Fawcett, T and Rhynas, S (2012) Taking a Patient History: The Role of the Nurse. *Nursing Standard*, 26(24): 41–8.

Fazio, S (2008) *The Enduring Self in People with Alzheimer's: Getting to the Heart of Individualized Care*. Baltimore, MD: Health Professions Press.

Festinger, L (1957/1985) A *Theory of Cognitive Dissonance*. Stanford, CA: Stanford University Press.

Fitzpatrick, S, Varma, S and Kuo, J (2020) Is Borderline Personality Disorder Really an Emotion Dysregulation Disorder and, If So, How? A Comprehensive Experimental Paradigm. *Psychological Medicine*, 52(12): 2319–31.

Foundation for People with Learning Disabilities (2018) *A Life Without Fear: A Call for Collective Action Against Learning Disability Hate Crime*. [online] Available at: www.learningdisabilities.org.uk/learning-disabilities/publications/life-without-fear (accessed 10 January 2023).

Francis, R (2013) *Report of the Mid Staffordshire NHS Foundation Trust Public Inquiry: Executive Summary*. [online] Available at: www.midstaffspublicinquiry.com/sites/default/files/report/Executive%20summary.pdf (accessed 23 February 2023).

Gluyas, H (2015) Patient-Centred Care: Improving Healthcare Outcomes. *Nursing Standard*, 30(4): 50–9.

Goffman, E (1963) *Stigma: Notes on the Management of Spoiled Identity*. London: Penguin Books.

Gold Standards Framework (2011) *The GSF Prognostic Indicator Guidance: The National GSF Centre's Guidance for Clinicians to Support Earlier Recognition of Patients Nearing the End of Life*. NHS End of Life Care Programme. [online] Available at: www.goldstandardsframework.org.uk (accessed 1 December 2022).

Gross, R (2020) *Psychology: The Science of Mind and Behaviour*. 8th ed. London: Hodder Education.

Grover, E, Porter, J and Morphet, J (2017) An Exploration of Emergency Nurses' Perceptions, Attitudes and Experience of Teamwork in the Emergency Department. *Australasian Emergency Nursing Journal*, 20(2): 92–7.

Hall, S and Melia, Y (2022) I Just Pulled Myself Together and Realised I Had to Be Responsible: Adolescents' Experiences of Having a Friend Who Self-harms. *Child & Youth Care Forum*, 51: 291–311.

Hamza, A, Stewart, S and Willoughby, T (2012) Examining the Link Between Non-suicidal Self-injury and Suicidal Behavior: A Review of the Literature and an Integrated Model. *Clinical Psychology Review*, 32(6): 482–95.

Hardy, S (2022) *Mental Health and Wellbeing: A Guide for Nurses and Healthcare Professionals Working with Adults in Primary Care.* Keswick: M&K Update Ltd.

Hart, C (2014) *A Pocket Guide to Risk Assessment and Management in Mental Health.* Abingdon: Routledge.

Health Foundation (2016) Implementing Shared Decision Making: Clinical Teams' Experiences of Implementing Shared Decision Making as part of the MAGIC Programme. [online] Available at: www. health.org.uk/publications/implementing-shared-decision-making (accessed 1 December 2022).

Henderson, S, Horne, M, Hills, R and Kendall, E (2018) Cultural Competence in Healthcare in the Community: A Concept Analysis. *Health & Social Care in the Community,* 26(4): 590–603.

Heron, J (1976) A Six-Category Intervention Analysis. *British Journal of Guidance and Counselling,* 4(2): 143–55.

Heron, J (2001) *Helping the Client: A Creative Practical Guide.* London: Sage.

Higgins, A, Morrissey, J, Doyle, L, Bailey, J and Gill, A (2015) *Best Practice Principles for Risk Assessment and Safety Planning for Nurses Working in Mental Health Services.* Dublin: Health Service Executive. [online] Available at: https://core.ac.uk/download/pdf/45263235.pdf (accessed 23 February 2023).

Hill, R (2021) Assessment, Planning, Implementation and Evaluation (APIE): The Process of Nursing. In Delves-Yates, C (ed) *Essentials of Nursing Practice* (pp 205–18). 3rd ed. London: Sage.

HM Government (2018) *Working Together to Safeguard Children.* London: HM Government.

Home Office (2015) *Statutory Guidance Framework: Controlling or Coercive Behaviour in an Intimate or Family Relationship.* [online] Available at: https://assets.publishing.service.gov.uk/government/ uploads/system/uploads/attachment_data/file/482528/Controllingor_coercivebehaviour_-statutory_ guidance.pdf (accessed 23 February 2023).

Home Office (2022) *Domestic Abuse: Statutory Guidance.* London: The Stationery Office. [online] Available at: https://assets.publishing.service.gov.uk/government/uploads/system/uploads/ attachment_data/file/1089015/Domestic_Abuse_Act_2021_Statutory_Guidance.pdf (accessed 23 February 2023).

Jackson, A (2021) *Dilemmas and Decision Making in Social Work.* St Albans: Critical Publishing.

Jacobs, M (2017). *Psychodynamic Counselling in Action.* Oxford: Sage.

Javaid, A, Nakata, V and Dasari, M (2019) Diagnostic Overshadowing in Learning Disability: Think Beyond the Disability. *Progress in Neurology and Psychiatry,* 23(2): 8–10.

Kelly, A (2018) *Working with Adults with a Learning Disability.* London: Routledge.

Kieling, C, Baker-Henningham, H, Belfer, M, Conti, G, Ertem, I, Omigbodun, O, Rohde, L A, Srinath, S, Ulkuer, N and Rahman, A (2011) Child and Adolescent Mental Health Worldwide: Evidence for Action. *The Lancet,* 378(9801): 1515–25.

Kitwood, T (1997) *Dementia Reconsidered: The Person Comes First*. Buckingham: Open University Press.

Klonsky, E D, Oltmanns, T F and Turkheimer, E (2003) Deliberate Self-harm in a Nonclinical Population: Prevalence and Psychological Correlates. *The American Journal of Psychiatry*, 160(8): 1501–8.

Kourkouta, L and Papathanasiou, I V (2014) Communication in Nursing Practice. *Materia Socio-Medica*, 26(1): 65–7.

Kubler-Ross, E (2014) *On Death and Dying: What the Dying Have to Teach Doctors, Nurses, Clergy and Their Families*. New York: Scribner.

Kubler-Ross, E and Kessler, D (2014) *On Grief and Grieving: Finding the Meaning of Grief Through the Five Stages of Loss*. London: Simon and Schuster.

Kuiper, R A (2016) *Clinical Reasoning and Care Coordination in Advanced Practice Nursing*. New York: Springer Publishing Company.

Lazarus, R (1999) Hope: An Emotion and a Vital Coping Resource Against Despair. *Social Research*, 66(2): 653–78.

Linehan, M M (1987) Dialectical Behavior Therapy for Borderline Personality Disorder: Theory and Method. *Bulletin of the Menninger Clinic*, 51(3): 261–76.

Linehan, M M (1993) *Cognitive-Behavioural Treatment of Borderline Personality Disorder*. New York: The Guilford Press.

Linehan, M M (2015) *DBT Skills Training Manual*. New York: Guilford Press.

Lirette, M, Ladha, Z, Principi, T and Beno, S (2018) Improving Communication in a Multidisciplinary Team Using Digital Monitors and a Handover Tool (ATMIST Mnemonic) During Paediatric Traumas. *British Medical Journal Leader*, 2: 6–7.

Ljungholm, L, Edin-Liljegren, A, Ekstedt, M and Klinga, C (2022). What Is Needed for Continuity of Care and How Can We Achieve It? – Perceptions Among Multiprofessionals on the Chronic Care Trajectory. *Biomed Central Health Services Research*, 22: 686.

Long, K, Kim, E, Chen, Y, Wilson, M, Everett, F, Worthington, L, Tyler, J and VanderWeele, J (2020) The Role of Hope in Subsequent Health and Well-being for Older Adults: An Outcome-Wide Longitudinal Approach. *Global Epidemiology*, 2.

Lott, C, Truhlá, A, Alfonzo, A, Barelli, A, González-Salvado, V, Hinkelbein, J, Nolan, J, Paal, P, Perkins, G, Thies, K, Yeung, J, Zideman, D and Soar, J (2021) European Resuscitation Council Guidelines 2021: Cardiac Arrest in Special Circumstances. *Resuscitation*, 161: 152–219.

Maslach, C (1999) A Multidimensional Theory of Burnout. In Cooper, C L (ed) *Theories of Organizational Stress* (pp 68–85). Oxford: Oxford University Press.

Mason-Angelou, V (2020) *This Is Us – This Is What We Do: A Report to Inform the Future of Learning Disability Nursing*. National Development Team for Inclusion. [online] Available at: www.ndti.org.uk/assets/files/Learning-Disability-Nursing-Report-FINAL.pdf (accessed 23 February 2023).

Mayer, J D and Salovey, P (1997) What Is Emotional Intelligence? In Salovey, P and Sluyter, D (eds) *Emotional Development and Emotional Intelligence: Educational Implications* (pp 3–31). New York: Basic Books.

McCartney, G, Popham, F, McMaster, R and Cumbers, A (2019) Defining Health and Health Inequalities. *Public Health*, 172: 22–30.

McCormack, B and McCance, T (eds) (2016). *Person-Centred Practice in Nursing and Health Care: Theory and Practice*. London: John Wiley & Sons.

McCormack, B, McCance, T, Bulley, C, Brown, D, McMillan, A and Martin, S (2021) *Person-Centred Healthcare Practice*. Hoboken, NJ: Wiley Blackwell.

McGovern, J (2015) Living Better with Dementia: Strengths-Based Social Work Practice and Dementia Care. *Social Work in Health Care*, 54(5): 408–21.

McKay, M, Wood, J and Brantley, J (2019) *The Dialectical Behavior Therapy Skills Workbook: Practical DBT Exercises for Learning Mindfulness, Interpersonal Effectiveness, Emotion Regulation, and Distress Tolerance*. 2nd ed. Oakland, CA: New Harbinger Publications.

McKenna, L, Innes, K, French, J, Streitberg, S and Gilmour, C (2011) Is History Taking a Dying Skill? An Exploration Using a Simulated Learning Environment. *Nurse Education in Practice*, 11(4): 234–8.

McKinnon, J (2018) In Their Shoes: An Ontological Perspective on Empathy in Nursing Practice. *Journal of Clinical Nursing*, 27(21–22): 3882–93.

Meitar, D and Karnieli-Miller, O (2022) Twelve Tips to Manage a Breaking Bad News Process: Using S-P-w-ICE-S – a Revised Version of the SPIKES Protocol. *Medical Teacher*, 44(10): 1087–91.

Melin-Johansson, C, Palmqvist, R and Rönnberg, L (2017) Clinical Intuition in the Nursing Process and Decision-Making: A Mixed-Studies Review. *Journal of Clinical Nursing*, 26 (23–24): 3936–49.

Mencap (2007) *Death by Indifference: 74 Deaths and Counting*. [online] Available at: www.mencap.org.uk/sites/ default/files/2016-08/Death%20by%20I ndifference%20-%2074%20deaths%20and%20counting.pdf (accessed 15 December 2022).

Mental Health Foundation (2021) Stigma and Discrimination. [online] Available at: www.mentalhealth.org.uk/a-to-z/s/stigma-and-discrimination (accessed 23 February 2023).

Mind (2020) Suicidal Feelings. [online] Available at: www.mind.org.uk/information-support/types-of-mental-healthproblems/suicidal-feelings/about-suicidal-feelings (accessed 23 February 2023).

Mishel, M and Clayton, M (2008) Theories of Uncertainty in Illness. In Smith, M J and Liehr, P (eds) *Middle Range Theory for Nursing* (pp 55–84). 2nd ed. New York: Springer.

Missah, S, Ostrowski, M and Heathcote, J (2008) Disease Progression in Chronic Hepatitis C: Modifiable and Nonmodifiable Factors. *Gastroenterology*, 134: 1699–714.

Mitchell, M, Coyer, F, Kean, S, Stone, R, Murfield, J and Dwan, T (2016) Patient, Family-Centred Care Interventions within the Adult ICU Setting: An Integrative Review. *Australian Critical Care*, 29(4): 179–93.

Molina-Mula, J and Gallo-Estrada, J (2020) Impact of Nurse-Patient Relationship on Quality of Care and Patient Autonomy in Decision-Making. *International Journal of Environmental Research and Public Health*, 17(3): 835.

Motz, A (2010) Self-harm as a Sign of Hope. *Psychoanalytic Psychotherapy*, 24(2): 81–92.

Moudatsou, M, Stavropoulou, A, Philalithis, A and Koukouli, S (2020) The Role of Empathy in Health and Social Care Professionals. *Healthcare*, 8(1): 26.

Mudallal, R H, Othman, W M and Al Hassan, N F (2017) Nurses' Burnout: The Influence of Leader Empowering Behaviors, Work Conditions, and Demographic Traits. *Inquiry*, 54. [online] Available at: www.ncbi.nlm.nih.gov/pmc/articles/PMC5798741/ (accessed 23 January 2023).

Nash, K, Bentley, I and Hirschfield, G (2009) Managing Hepatitis C Virus Infection. *British Medical Journal*, 339: 37–42.

National Institute for Health and Care Excellence (NICE) (2015) *Violence and Aggression: Short-Term Management in Mental Health, Health, and Community Settings.* London: British Psychological Society. [online] Available at: www.nice.org.uk/guidance/ng10 (accessed 23 February 2023).

National Institute for Health and Care Excellence (NICE) (2016) *Transition from Children's to Adults' Services for Young People Using Health or Social Care Services.* NG43. [online] Available at: www.nice.org.uk/guidance/ng43/chapter/Recommendations (accessed 23 February 2023).

National Institute for Health and Care Excellence (NICE) Guidelines (2019) Shared Decision Making. [online] Available at: www.nice.org.uk/about/what-we-do/our-programmes/nice-guidance/nice-guidelines/shared-decision-making (accessed 23 February 2023).

National Institute for Health and Care Excellence (NICE) (2020) Suspected Cancer: Recognition and Referral. [online] Available at: www.nice.org.uk/guidance/ng12 (accessed 23 February 2023).

National Institute for Health and Care Excellence NICE (2021) Scenario: Assessment of Pain. [online] Available at: https://cks.nice.org.uk/topics/palliative-cancer-care-pain/management/assessment-of-pain (accessed 23 February 2023).

National Institute for Health and Care Excellence (NICE) (nd) Multiple Long-Term Conditions. [online] Available at: www.nice.org.uk/guidance/conditions-and-diseases/multiple-long-term-conditions (accessed 23 January 2023).

National Institute for Health and Care Research (2021) Why We Need More Inclusive Research. [online] Available at: https://evidence.nihr.ac.uk/collection/why-we-need-more-inclusive-research (accessed 23 February 2023).

National Society for the Prevention of Cruelty to Children (NSPCC) (2020) *Domestic Abuse: Learning from Case Reviews*. [online] Available at: https://learning.nspcc.org.uk/media/1335/learning-from-case-reviews_domestic-abuse.pdf (accessed 23 February 2023).

National Society for the Prevention of Cruelty to Children (NSPCC) (2022) Learning: Gillick Competency and Fraser Guidelines. [online] Available at: https://learning.nspcc.org.uk/child-protection-system/gillick-competence-fraser-guidelines (accessed 29 November 2022).

NHS (2019) Consent to Treatment: Overview. [online] Available at: www.nhs.uk/conditions/consent-to-treatment (accessed 23 February 2023).

NHS (2020) Advance Decision to Refuse Treatment (Living Will). [online] Available at: www.nhs.uk/conditions/end-of-life-care/advance-decision-to-refuse-treatment (accessed 23 February 2023).

NHS (2022a). Hepatitis C. [online] Available at: www.nhs.uk/conditions/hepatitis-c/treatment (accessed 23 February 2023).

NHS (2022b) Beating Burnout in the NHS. [online] Available at: www.nhsemployers.org/articles/beating-burnout-nhs (accessed 23 February 2023).

NHS England (2017) *Introducing the 6Cs*. [online] Available at: www.england.nhs.uk/6cs/wp-content/uploads/sites/25/2015/03/introducing-the-6cs.pdf (accessed 5 January 2023).

NHS England (2019) NHS Long Term Plan. [online] Available at: www.longtermplan.nhs.uk (accessed 14 December 2023).

NHS England and NHS Improvement (2019) *The NHS Patient Safety Strategy: Safer Culture, Safer Systems, Safer Patients*. [online] Available at: www.england.nhs.uk/wp-content/uploads/2020/08/190708_Patient_Safety_Strategy_for_website_v4.pdf (accessed 23 February 2023).

NHS England and NHS Improvement (nd a) *Using Five Whys to Review a Simple Problem*. [online] Available at: www.england.nhs.uk/wp-content/uploads/2022/02/qsir-using-five-whys-to-review-a-simple-problem.pdf (accessed 5 January 2023).

NHS England and NHS Improvement (nd b) *SBAR Communication Tool −Situation, Background, Assessment, Recommendation*. [online] Available at: www.england.nhs.uk/wp-content/uploads/2021/03/qsir-sbar-communication-tool.pdf (accessed 5 January 2023).

Nibbelink, C W and Brewer B B (2018) Decision-Making in Nursing Practice: An Integrative Literature Review. *Journal of Clinical Nursing*, 27: 917–28.

Norah Fry Centre (2021) *Learning Disabilities Mortality Review (LeDeR) Programme (2020)*. Annual Report. Bristol: University of Bristol. [online] Available at: https://leder.nhs.uk/images/annual_reports/LeDeR-bristol-annual-report-2020.pdf (accessed 15 December 2022).

Nursing and Midwifery Council (NMC) (2016) *Enabling Professionalism in Nursing and Midwifery Practice*. [online] Available at: www.nmc.org.uk/globalassets/sitedocuments/other-publications/enabling-professionalism.pdf (accessed 23 February 2023).

Nursing and Midwifery Council (NMC) (2018a) *Future Nurse: Standards of Proficiency for Registered Nurses*. [online] Available at: www.nmc.org.uk/standards/standards-for-nurses/standards-of-proficiency-for-registered-nurses/ (accessed 12 December 2022).

Nursing and Midwifery Council (NMC) (2018b) *The Code: Professional Standards of Practice and Behaviour for Nurses, Midwives and Nursing Associates*. London: Nursing & Midwifery Council.

Nursing and Midwifery Council (NMC) (2019) *Regulators Unite to Support Reflective Practice Across Health and Care*. [online] Available at: www.nmc.org.uk/news/press-releases/joint-statement-reflective-practice (accessed 23 February 2023).

Nursing and Midwifery Council (NMC) (nd) *Delegation and Accountability: Supplementary Information to the NMC Code*. [online] Available at: www.nmc.org.uk/globalassets/sitedocuments/ nmc-publications/ delegation-and-accountability-supplementary-information-to-the-nmc-code.pdf (accessed 23 January 2023).

Oates, J R and Maani-Fogelman, P A (2022) *Nursing Grief and Loss*. Treasure Island, FL: StatPearls Publishing.

Oxtoby, K (2020) How Unconscious Bias Can Discriminate Against Patients and Affect Their Care. *British Medical Journal*, 2020: 371.

Patel, K M and Metersky, K (2022) Reflective Practice in Nursing: A Concept Analysis. *International Journal of Nursing Knowledge*, 33(3): 180–7.

Paterick, Z, Paterick, T E and Paterick, B B (2020) Medical Informed Choice: Understanding the Element of Time to Meet the Standard of Care for Valid Informed Consent. *Postgrad Medical Journal*, 96(1141): 708–10.

Pendleton, D, Schofield, T and Tate, P (2003) *The New Consultation: Developing Doctor–Patient Communication*. Oxford: Oxford University Press.

Powell, T (2013) *The Francis Report (Report of the Mid-Staffordshire NHS Foundation Trust Public Inquiry) and the Government's Response*. [online] Available at: https://researchbriefings.files.parliament. uk/documents/SN06690/SN06690.pdf (accessed 23 February 2023).

Puffer, R, Yue, J, Mesley, M, Billigen, J, Sharpless, J, Fetzick, A, Puccio, A, Diaz-Arrastia, R and Okonkwo, D (2018) Long-Term Outcome in Traumatic Brain Injury Patients with Midline Shift: A Secondary Analysis of the Phase 3 COBRIT Clinical Trial. *Journal of Neurosurgery*, 131(2): 596–603.

Quill, T and Cassel, C (1995) Nonabandonment: A Central Obligation for Physicians. *Annals of Internal Medicine*, 122(5): 368–74.

Rahilly, T and Hendry, E (eds) (2014) *Promoting the Wellbeing of Children in Care: Messages from Research* (pp 241–56). London: NSPCC.

Resuscitation Council UK (2015) *The ABCDE Approach*. London: Resuscitation Council UK. [online] Available at: www.resus.org.uk/library/2015-resuscitation-guidelines/abcde-approach (accessed 23 February 2023).

Resuscitation Council UK (2020) *ReSPECT*. 3rd ed. [online] Available at: www.resus.org.uk/respect/ respect-resources (accessed 23 February 2023).

Resuscitation Council UK (2021a) Ethics Guidelines. [online] Available at: www.resus.org.uk/library/2021-resuscitation-guidelines/ethics-guidelines (accessed 12 January 2023).

Resuscitation Council UK (2021b) Paediatric Advanced Life Support Guidelines. [online] Available at: www.resus.org.uk/library/2021-resuscitation-guidelines/paediatric-advanced-life-support-guidelines (accessed 23 January 2023).

Rogers, C (1979) The Foundations of the Person-Centred Approach. *Education*, 1001(2): 98–107.

Royal College of Nursing (2010) Principles of Nursing Practice. [online] Available at: www.rcn.org.uk/professional-development/publications/pub-003864 (accessed 23 February 2023).

Sastrawan, S, Newton, J M and Malik, G (2019) Nurses' Integrity and Coping Strategies: An Integrative Review. *Journal of Clinical Nursing*, 28(5–6): 733–44.

Schnider, A (2012) Confabulation in Reality Filtering. In Ramachandran, V S (ed) *Encyclopedia of Human Behavior* (pp 563–71). 2nd ed. Cambridge, MA: Elsevier.

Sedig, L (2016) Care When Patients and Family Members Don't Agree? *American Medical Association Journal of Ethics*, 18(1): 12–17.

Selder, F (1989) Life Transition Theory: The Resolution of Uncertainty. *Nursing and Health Care*, 10(8): 437–51.

Self-injury Support (nd) Harm Minimisation. [online] Available at: www.selfinjurysupport.org.uk/pages/faqs/category/harm-minimisation (accessed 23 February 2023).

Shaw, K, Ritchie, D and Adams, G (2011) Does Witnessing Resuscitation Help Parents Come to Terms with the Death of their Child? A Review of the Literature. *Intensive and Critical Care Nursing*, 27(5): 253–62.

Shepherd, M (2012) *Every Contact Counts: A Review of the Evidence*. Public Health Wales. [online] Available at: www.msresearch.co.uk/resources/Every%20contact%20counts.pdf (accessed 23 February 2023).

Shepherd, S M (2019) Cultural Awareness Workshops: Limitations and Practical Consequences. *BMC Medical Education*, 19(1): 1–10.

Sherwood, G, Cherian, U K, Horton-Deutsch, S, Kitzmiller, R and Smith-Miller, C (2022) Reflective Practices: Meaningful Recognition for Healthy Work Environments. *Nursing Management*, 29(4): 30–4.

Sibiya, M (2018) Effective Communication in Nursing. In Ulutasdemir, N (ed) *Nursing* (Chapter 3). IntechOpen. [online] Available at: www.intechopen.com/chapters/59779 (accessed 23 February 2023).

Sidebotham, P, Brendon, M, Bailey, S, Belderson, P, Dodsworth, J, Garstang, J, Harrison, E, Retzer, A and Sorenson, P (2016) *Pathways to Protection: A Triennial Analysis of Serious Case Reviews 2011 to 201, Final Report*. London, Department of Education.

Silva, A, Arora, S, Dhanani, S, Hornby, L, Luctkar-Flude, M, Ross-White, A, Lotherington, K, Rochon, A, Wilson, L, Latifi, M, Giorno, L and Silva e Silva, V (2022) Quality Improvement Tools to Manage Deceased Organ Donation Processes: A Scoping Review Protocol. *Nurse Education in Practice*, 61: 103322.

Silverman, J, Kurtz, S and Draper J (2013) *Skills for Communicating with Patients*. 3rd ed. London: Routledge.

Silvers, J A (2022) Adolescence as a Pivotal Period for Emotion Regulation Development. *Current Opinion in Psychology*, 44: 258–63.

Slater, A (2019) Exploring the Implementation of Family-Witnessed Resuscitation in Children and Young People. *Nursing Children and Young People*, 31(6): 32–5.

Smikle, M (2018) Safeguarding Children: Providing Nursing Staff with Supervision. *Nursing Times*, 114(12): 36–40.

Snyder, C (2002) Hope Theory: Rainbows in the Mind. *Psychological Inquiry*, 13(4): 249–75.

Social Care Institute for Excellence (SCIE) (2016) The Care Act: Safeguarding Adults. [online] Available at: www.scie.org.uk/care-act-2014/safeguarding-adults (accessed: 13 January 2023).

Social Care Institute for Excellence (SCIE) (2020) Types and Indicators of Abuse. [online] Available at: www.scie.org.uk/safeguarding/adults/introduction/types-and-indicators-of-abuse (accessed 13 January 2023).

Social Care Institute for Excellence (SCIE) (2022) Mental Capacity Act 2005 at a Glance. [online] Available at: www.scie.org.uk/mca/introduction/mental-capacity-act-2005-at-a-glance (accessed 13 January 2023).

Stark, E (2007) *Coercive Control: How Men Entrap Women in Personal Life*. New York: Oxford University Press.

Stark, E and Hester, M (2018) Coercive Control: Update and Review. *Violence Against Women*, 25(1): 81–104.

Stenhouse, R (2021) Understanding Equality and Diversity in Nursing Practice. *Nursing Standard (Royal College of Nursing (Great Britain)*, 36(2): 27–33.

Su, J, Masika, G, Paguio, J and Redding, S (2020) Defining Compassionate Nursing Care. *Nursing Ethics*, 27(2): 480–93.

Suhd, M M (1995) *Positive Regard: Carl Rogers and Other Notables He Influenced*. Palo Alto, CA: Science and Behavior Books.

Taberna, M, Gil Moncayo, F, Jané-Salas, E, Antonio, M, Arribas, L, Vilajosana, E, Peralvez Torres, E and Mesía, R (2020) The Multidisciplinary Team Approach and Quality of Care. *Frontiers in Oncology*, 10: 85.

Telford, K, Kralik, D and Koch, T (2006) Acceptance and Denial: Implications for People Adapting to Chronic Illness: Literature Review. *Journal of Advanced Nursing*, 55(4): 457–64.

Thacker, H, Ankar, A and Penhale, B (2019) Could Curiosity Save Lives? An Exploration into the Value of Employing Professional Curiosity and Partnership Work in Safeguarding Adults under the Care Act 2014. *The Journal of Adult Protection*, 21(5): 252–67.

Thompson, N (2018) *Mental Health and Well-being: Alternatives to the Medical Model.* Abingdon: Routledge.

Tilburt, J, James, K, Sinicrope, P, Eton, D, Costello, B, Carey, J, Lane, M, Ehlers, S, Erwin, P, Nowakowski, K and Murad, M (2011) Factors Influencing Cancer Risk Perception in High-Risk Populations: A Systematic Review. *Hereditary Cancer in Clinical Practice*, 9(1): 1–15.

Tracy, G (2013) How Nurses Can Encourage Shared Decision Making. *Nursing*, 43(8): 65–6.

UKRI (Research and Innovation) (2022) Consent. [online] Available at: www.ukri.org/councils/esrc/guidance-for-applicants/research-ethics-guidance (accessed 23 February 2023).

Varkey, B (2021) Principles of Clinical Ethics and Their Application to Practice. *Medical Principles and Practice*, 30: 17–28.

Veesart, A and Barron, A (2020) Unconscious Bias: Is It Impacting Your Nursing Care? *Nursing Made Incredibly Easy!* 18(2): 47–9.

Wheaton, A (2022) Balancing Honesty and Benevolence in Dementia Care: A Commentary on Therapeutic Lies and Codes of Ethics. *Journal of Nursing Management*, 30(7): 2241–4.

Wilde, B (2023) Multicultural Societies: Diversity, Discrimination and Social Inclusion. In Stanley, S (ed) *Contemporary Social Problems in the UK* (pp 255–77). Abingdon, Routledge.

Wiseman, P and Watson, N (2022) 'Because I've Got a Learning Disability, They Don't Take Me Seriously': Violence, Wellbeing, and Devaluing People with Learning Disabilities. *Journal of Interpersonal Violence*, 37(13/14).

World Health Organization (WHO) (2010) *User Empowerment in Mental Health – a Statement by the WHO Regional Office for Europe.* [online] Available at: www.euro.who.int/__data/assets/pdf_file/0020/113834/E93430.pdf (accessed 23 February 2023).

World Health Organization (WHO) (2012) WHOQOL: Measuring Quality of Life. [online] Available at: www.who.int/tools/whoqol (accessed 23 February 2023).

World Health Organization (WHO) (2017) *Hepatitis C: Global Hepatitis Report.* [online] Available at: www.who.int/publications/i/item/9789241565455 (accessed 23 February 2023).

World Health Organization (WHO) (2020) *Guidelines on Mental Health Promotive and Preventive Interventions for Adolescents.* [online] Available at: www.who.int/docs/default-source/mental-health/guidelines-on-mental-health-promotive-and-preventive-interventions-for-adolescents-hat.pdf?sfvrsn=3db4085b_2 (accessed 23 February 2023).

World Health Organization (WHO) (2022). Hepatitis C. [online] Available at: www.who.int/news-room/fact-sheets/detail/hepatitis-c (accessed 23 February 2023).

Wright, K M (2021) Exploring the Therapeutic Relationship in Nursing Theory and Practice. *Mental Health Practice.* [online] Available at: https://clok.uclan.ac.uk/37860/1/37859%20Wright%20KM%202021%2520Therapeutic%20relationship%20CPD%20MHP%20accepted%2012thApril2021.pdf (accessed 3 April 2023).

Index

7 Golden Rules of Information Sharing, 32

ABCDE assessment, 8, 14, 60
abuse, recognising signs of, 26, 32, *See also* domestic abuse; sexual abuse
acceptance, 110, 132–3
of loss, 151, 155
psychological, 135
accountability, 17, 20–1
accurate documentation/record keeping, 9, 13, 29, 91, 92, 98
act without delay clause, 18, 21
active listening, 37, 48–9, 52, 78, 96, 140
and communication, 101, 130, 131
requirements, 135, 144
and respect, 44, 54, 86, 111, 135
for understanding, 130
adolescent mental health, 119, 124
advance care plan, 141, 145
advance directive, 141, 145
adverse childhood experiences (ACEs), 12, 13, 103, 111–12
advocacy, 36, 43, 61, 64, 72, 74, 152, 155
aggressive behaviour, 18
alternative perspectives, 37, 42
altruism, 69, 74
analgesic ladder for cancer pain, 141, 146
anchoring bias, 167
aphasia in dementia, 78, 84
assertive communication, 61, 65
assessment, 89, 90, 91, 92, 96
of mental/physical safety, 91, 97–8

wound care, 97
assessment/coma scale, 90, 97
assumptions, 27, 30
assumptions, making, 38, 42
ATMIST handover, 60, 65
attachment, separation, 103, 112
authority bias, 167
autonomy, promoting, 132, 134
availability heuristic, 167

behaviourism, 104, 115
bereavement stages, 129, 130, 134
bias, 49, 53
biomedical model, 37, 44, 106, 116
biosocial model, 104, 115
blind spot bias, 167
brief encounters/every contact counts, 91, 99
burnout, 102, 111, 140, 145

Calgary Cambridge Communication Model, 139, 146
cancer prevalence and risk perception, 127, 129, 134
care, 41
and compassion, 36
-coordination, 102, 115
efficient and effective, 101, 109
planning, 130, 135
Care Act (2014), 18, 21
caring, 77, 83, 106, 110, 149, 154
cervical spine immobilisation, 90, 97
Charter for Planning Ahead, 141, 145
child protection, 27, 31

child-centred approach to safeguarding, 11, 13
Children Act 1989, 32
children's social care (CSC), 27
chronic illness, 131, 132, 135
clarification questions, 120, 125
clinical supervision, 104, 115
clustering illusion, 167
coercive control, 11, 13, 18, 19, 21, 26, 28, 31
cognitive dissonance theory, 102, 111
cognitive impairment, 79, 85, 150, 155
collaborative risk management, 39, 43
collaborative working, 81
commitment, 37, 41
communication, 77, 92, 95, 101, 119, 124, 128, 130, 158, 159
and active listening, 101, 130, 131
assertive, 72, 75
in dementia, assumptions about, 77, 83
in dementia care, 85
effective, 28, 46, 47, 52, 53, 69, 75, 134
importance of, 109, 134, 155
non-verbal, 157
open questioning, 92, 140, 150
positive, 79, 86
in sexual health, 164
skills, 30
SPIKES model, 128, 133, 136, 138, 139, 146
of unmet need, 77, 83
use of humour, 91

compassion, 78, 138, 152, 157, 158, 164
  and care, 61, 64
  definition of, 109–41, 143–4
competence, 26, 30, 77, 83, 110–83
compliance with social norms, 112
confidentiality, 15, 20, 46, 49, 52, 69
  importance of, 74
  moral obligation of, 48, 53
  and safeguarding, 158, 164
confirmation, 92, 95
confirmation bias, 167
conflict avoidance, 150, 155–6
confusion in the ward environment, 78, 84
consent, 27, 28, 31, 45, See also informed consent; valid consent
conservatism bias, 167
consultation skills, 158, 165
contempt, 102
continuity of care, 140, 146
contraceptive consultation, 159, 160, 161, 165
contraceptive methods, choice of, 160, 161, 162, 164
controlling behaviour, 25, 28, 30
coping mechanisms, 103, 112
counselling, 92, 99, 120, 125
courage, 26, 30, 104, 110–41
cultural awareness, 120, 123
cultural competencies, 120, 125
culturally informed practice, 37, 44, 79, 84
curiosity, 37, 43, 78, 83, 150, 154
cycle of repeated abuse, 27, 31

Daffodil Standards, 142, 145
decision-making pitfalls, 167
de-escalation, 26, 32
delegation, 16, 22
dementia syndrome, 149, 156
diagnostic overshadowing, 18, 19, 21, 90, 95
dialectical behaviour therapy (DBT), 102, 103–4, 105, 106, 114
dialectics, 106, 113
differential coping, 141, 144
disabling social environments, 79, 84
disclosure, 49, 50, 53
disorientation, 78
disorientation for time and place, 150, 155
distraction, 105, 114
distraction/questioning, 92, 94
distressed behaviours, 16, 21
distributive justice, 70–1, 75
domestic abuse, 12, 26, 31, 40, 121, 126
drug and alcohol intoxication, 89, 99
Duluth wheel of power and control, 26, 32
duty of care to safeguard, 28, 30

echoing, 92, 99
emotion dysregulation, 104, 112
emotional abuse, 27, 31
emotional intelligence, 19, 21
emotional overwhelm, 103, 112
emotional regulation, 103, 106, 112
empathy, 25, 71, 92, 95, 138, 157, 158, 164

definition of, 74, 109–41, 143–4
significance of, 29
and understanding, 37, 78
empowerment, 132, 135
environmental stressors, 78, 84
ethical decision making, 61, 65
ethical principles, 141, 145
ethical research, 45, 47, 48, 49, 50, 52, 54

family-centred care, 9, 13
fear, 102
Fraser Guidelines, 43, 165
freedom to choose, 39, 42

gaining trust through play, 8, 13
general sexual health advice, 160
getting to know the person, 91, 95
group think bias, 167

harm minimisation, 107, 114
health beliefs, 37, 42
health check, 16
health education, 103, 114
health inequalities, 16, 17, 19, 21
health promotion, 48, 54
health review, 22
'hello, my name is' campaign, 8, 13, 46, 53, 102, 110, 134, 139, 149, 154
history taking, 90, 96–7, 101, 113, 119, 124, 138, 146
honesty, 48, 50, 53, 150, 154
hope, 131, 132, 135
humour, use of, 91, 95

identity, 152, 155
inclusive research, 50, 54
information and
    education, 36, 43
information sharing, 27, 29, 31
informed choice, 141, 144
informed consent, 45, 54,
    140, 146
inner conflict, 150, 155
inter-agency working,
    89, 90, 96
inter-professional working,
    90, 97
intuition, 7, 8, 13, 35, 36, 40,
    43, 90

judgements and assumptions,
    101, 109

knowing, forms of, 90, 96

last year of life, identification
    of being in, 138, 144
learning disability nurse, role
    of, 15, 22
life history and life story,
    150, 155
lighthouse leadership, 59, 65
looked after children, working
    with, 103, 113–14
loss and the grief response,
    104, 112, 140, 145

malignant social psychology,
    79, 92
MDT working, 104, 115
medical justice, 70, 75
Medical Model, The,
    102, 115
memory, 150, 152, 156
Mental Capacity Act (2005),
    16, 17, 21

misidentification in dementia,
    149, 154
modelling best practice,
    79, 86
multi-agency working, 27, 32
multi-cultural society,
    119, 125
multidisciplinary teams,
    15, 22, 102, 113, 138,
    140, 146

NHS Long Term Plan, 2
NMC standards, 1–2
nonabandonment, 63, 65
non-directive nursing
    practice, 38, 43
non-judgemental care, 37, 43,
    52, 53, 102, 110, 160,
    161, 164
non-maleficence, 73, 75,
    150, 155
non-threatening body language,
    92, 98
non-verbal communication, 38,
    42, 78, 86, 157
nurses acting as advocates,
    152, 155

observation skills, 78, 85
observational assessment, 35,
    42, 119, 120, 124
open questioning, 28,
    31, 92, 95
open-minded practice,
    37, 43
openness and
    transparency, 71, 74
organisational cultures,
    102, 111
ostrich effect, 167
outpacing, 79, 84–5
over-optimism, 167

paediatric advanced life
    support, 60, 65
pain assessment tools,
    138, 146
paramountcy, 27, 32
parasympathetic nervous
    system, 105, 113
patience, 67, 74
patient- and family-centred
    care, 68, 75
patient choice, 39, 41
patient empowerment,
    105, 110
patient safety, 67, 75, 105, 114
person behind the dementia,
    recognising, 80, 85
person/patient-centred care,
    101, 109, 119, 127, 128,
    131, 135, 137, 143, 150,
    153, 156
person-centred practice, 35, 43,
    91, 123, 152
person-centredness,
    91, 96, 99
person-focused
    communication, 38, 44
person-focused versus task-
    focused care, 80, 81, 86
physical violence, 11
physiology, 91, 96
poor diagnostic practice, 18
positive person work,
    80, 92
positive regard, 37, 43
positive risk taking, 104, 114
pre-hospital care, 89, 96
prejudice, 91, 94
prevention, 101, 115
principles of
    safeguarding, 39, 44
privacy and dignity, 140, 144
problem identification, 19, 23

professional curiosity, 16, 22

professional integrity, 150, 154

professional obligation, 48

professionalism, 26, 30, 47, 48, 53, 103, 110, 140, 144

psychodynamic principles, 120, 125

psychodynamic psychotherapy, 120, 124

quality of life, 140, 141, 144

raising concerns, 27, 30

reality orientation, 150, 155

reality, different perspectives on, 150, 155

recency bias, 167

record keeping, 29, 30, 91, 107, 110

reducing health inequalities, 16

referrals, timely, 16, 20

reflective practice, 80, 86, 92, 99, 107, 114, 140, 146, 151, 156

relationships and trust building, 47, 54

repetition bias, 167

repetitive vocalisations in dementia, 77, 83–4

resolving conflict, 77, 85

resource bias, 167

respect, 38, 43, 151, 154

ReSPECT form, 141, 145

revolving door syndrome, 101, 111

risk assessment, 104, 114

risk management, 104, 113

safeguarding, 121, 122, 126, 158, 159, 163, 165

safeguarding children, 10, 11, 13

safeguarding clinical supervision, 27, 32

safety planning, 104, 113

safety procedures at work, 120, 125

SBAR communication, 15, 22–3

scope of practice, 92, 98

self-care, 107, 115

self-care indicators, 92, 98

self-harm, 102, 111, 121, 126

self-harm as emotional regulation, 104, 113

self-injury and self-help versus future risk, 104, 113

self-reflection, 119, 123

self-soothing, 105, 113

sense-making, 149, 155

separation, 103

Serious Crime Act 2015, 40

sexual abuse, 121, 126

sexual history, 158, 162, 165

sexual violence, 11

shame, 37, 42

shared decision-making, 39, 42, 141, 146

similarity bias, 167

social and emotional development, 103, 115

social norms, compliance with, 103, 112

social stigma, 105, 113

socialisation, 103, 112

socio-economic determinants of health, 16, 21

SPIKES communication model, 128, 133, 136, 138, 139, 146

spiritual abuse, 39, 42

S-P-w-ICE-S model, 68, 75

stages of dementia, 78, 86

standing in their shoes, 78, 86

stereotyping, 36, 41–2

stigma, 49, 53

strengths-based nursing, 78, 81, 84

stress and distress in dementia, 77, 83

suicidal ideation, 92, 99–100

sunk-costs bias, 167

supported nutrition and hydration, need for, 77, 85

symptom management, 137, 145

system failure, 12

targeting by criminals, 18

teamwork, 8, 13

technical know-how, 90, 99

therapeutic lying, 150, 154

therapeutic relationships, 9, 13, 102, 111, 137, 139, 144

'This Is Me' document, 80, 81, 86

total pain, 143, 145

transference, 119, 124

transitions in care, 51, 54, 101, 110–11, 130, 131, 132, 135

trauma-informed care, 101, 113

uncertainty, 131, 132, 135

unconditional positive regard, 103, 107, 110

unconscious bias, 9, 13, 48, 53, 91, 94

United Kingdom Medical Eligibility Criteria for Contraceptive Use (UKMEC) Guidelines, 161

unpaid carers, recognising the need for support for, 105, 114

valid consent, 69, 75

validation, 103, 114, 131, 135, 150, 153, 155

vulnerability, 28, 31

vulnerable adults, 39, 40, 42

well-being, 168

well-being in dementia, 149, 154

witnessed resuscitation, 59, 65

wound care, 91